MORE WALKS TO
YORKSHIRE WATERFALLS

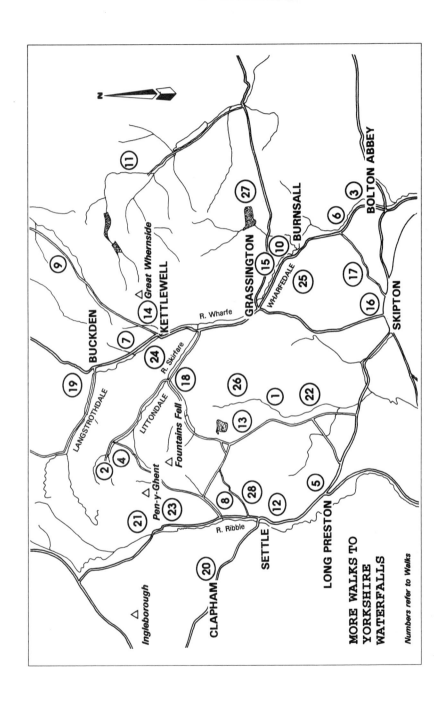

MORE WALKS TO
YORKSHIRE
WATERFALLS

Numbers refer to Walks

MORE WALKS TO
YORKSHIRE WATERFALLS

by

MARY WELSH

Illustrated by

LINDA WATERS

CICERONE PRESS
MILNTHORPE, CUMBRIA

MORE WALKS TO YORKSHIRE WATERFALLS
© Mary Welsh 1992
ISBN 1 85284 091 9

'Beech mast lie scattered' (*Page 33*)

CONTENTS

'this old walled track is a joy to walk'
Bark Lane, Heugh Gill. (Page 91)

PREFACE

This is a companion to my earlier book of walks to Yorkshire waterfalls. In this volume I have written of waterfalls to be found south of a line from Ingleton, through Buckden and on into Coverdale. Some of the falls, breathtaking in their magnificence, are well known and often visited. Others, maybe not so spectacular, have an elegance or gentle charm of their own.

The Dales have held me in their thrall for many years, but I need a purpose to my walks, and finding a waterfall has been that purpose. It has become an all-consuming passion to seek falls hidden in lush hollows, enfolded on high fells, sheltered in dense woodland or descending into deep pot holes in the midst of glorious limestone country. I hope you too, will be drawn back, time and time again, to seek out the waterfalls of the Dales.

For each waterfall I have devised a circular walk along existing rights of way. I have walked throughout the year and have described the birds, trees, flowers and other types of vegetation seen. I have written of artefacts of days gone by and of the present that are encountered along the way.

The sketch maps accompanying each walk are a general guide. The relevant OS maps (Outdoor Leisure 2, 10 and 30) should be used to locate the exact route. Wear suitable clothes and boots. Carry a compass, a whistle, some spare food and clothing. The weather can change rapidly and the high fells can become extremely cold.

My thanks go to my friends Maureen Fleming, Joan Morgan and Jane Hannah, who have helped me, so patiently, to research the walks. I would also like to thank Linda Waters, who has illustrated this second book with such a sure and true touch, enhancing all I have written.

Lastly, I must mention my faithful border collie, Cammie, who continues, in spite of her advancing years, to enjoy finding waterfalls as much as I do.

Good walking! Good waterfalling!

Janet's Foss

1. Janet's Foss and Waterfalls at Gordale Scar

MR 913634 - 916641, 4 miles

PARK IN THE large car park on the outskirts of Malham village. Walk through the main street, quiet now in January but full of visitors in the summer. By the bridge that carries the road over Malham Beck a dipper stands on a submerged rock and bobs and dips for food quite undisturbed by the passing cars or the tourist standing close by. Once over the bridge turn right, walking beside the beck where mallard pairs stay close together. The path leads to a stile, beyond which the well-made path continues beside the racing water. Climb the next stile and, moving away from Malham Beck, walk to the signpost, beside another stile, pointing the way to Janet's Foss. The next stile, beside a barn, gives access to a path that keeps close by a wall with open pasture to the left. Look for the large yellow waymarks to help you find the route through the many stiles at the start of the walk.

At the end of the field a ladder stile leads to a walled lane. Keeping close to Gordale Beck, cross to the stile ahead. Most of the stiles are in pairs and these wooden ladders protect the walls

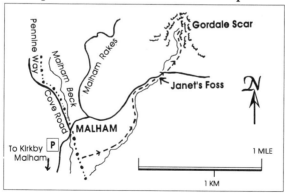

from the innumerable people who enjoy this walk in the summer months. Today the path is deserted; that is, except for the birds. A dipper repeatedly runs into the beck. A goldcrest fearlessly comes close to your head as it meticulously inspects each branch of a hawthorn. Its tiny pointed beak probes minute crevices in the bark, hunting for overwintering insects. It darts rapidly along the branches, ignoring the bounteous crop of haws. It comes so close that its chrome-yellow head is clear to see and all the time it si, si, sis quietly to itself. A wren, low on a branch close to the dipper, sings loudly and melodiously, and then another sings further along the river bank. On the other side of the water a flock of fieldfare crowds a line of tall ash. Had these birds been feeding on the haws ignored by the goldcrest?

Follow the path as it moves away from the water and comes close to a barn. Beyond, a crow picks up a rotten stick and drops it. It taps it and pecks it until it breaks, enabling the bird to feed on the insects inside. Climb the stiles ahead and walk on along the good path that now hugs the bank of the graceful, curving beck. Away on the other side a male kestrel sits atop an ash. It remains still for a long time and then wings its way towards the village.

The path, a pleasure to walk along, comes once again to more stiles, leaving the open pasture behind. The ground slopes upwards on both sides, with the beck and the path running along the bottom. A gate ahead leads into the wooded gorge sometimes called Little Gordale. The steep limestone sides are clad with sycamore, beech, wych elm, ash and hawthorn and from high up in one of the trees a green woodpecker 'laughs' but keeps itself well hidden. The woodland floor is very green with leaves of bramble, ivy, dog's mercury and herb robert. And then the path

Fieldfare

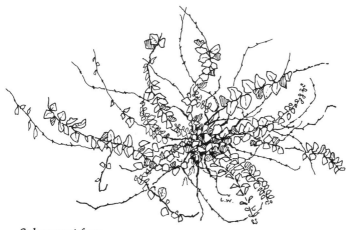

Spleenwort fern

climbs up a slope and Janet's Foss lies ahead.

Foss is the old Norse word for waterfall, and Janet was supposed to be the queen of the local fairies. Legend says that she lives in a small cave behind the falling water. Gordale Beck tumbles over a tufa screen, the tufa formed as lime-rich water breaks over the mossy edge of the fall. Calcite deposited over the moss gradually petrifies it, forming an apron of rock from the lip of the fall into the pool beneath. The beck divides into two main jets, and there is a small side fall; all three fall into a wide blue-green pool below. Ferns, including spleenwort, grow in profusion round the pool and herb robert still flowers.

Walk on up the path to a gate onto the road. Turn right, noticing the old narrow bridge that carried the road before it was widened. Twenty yards on, on the left, lies the gate to the path that leads into the gorge of Gordale. The magnificent limestone sides tower upwards and as the walker moves into their shadow the valley between narrows. Through the valley Gordale Beck dances and chuckles on its way, its bed bright green with cress growing in great masses. Ash, hawthorn and yew are scattered thinly over the towering slopes and overhead jackdaws perform an aerial ballet in the rising air current. The path takes you deeper into the narrowing, darkening gorge and then it winds round a buttress of rock and the spectacular waterfalls lie ahead.

11

High on the very edge of the gorge an ash hangs over the enormous ravine and in this leafless tree sit more jackdaws. Regularly they glide over the abyss from one side to the other and then sit, as if curious about those minute humans below.

The noise of the falling water echoes from the limestone faces, then reverberates from side to side. The top waterfall gushes through a hole in the rock high up. Once debris blocked this aperture, forming a deep but narrow lake in the valley above the fall. Apparently in 1730 a violent flood broke through the debris and diverted the stream to its present course. Below, the beck then falls in two magnificent jets over more tufa formed by large quantities of limestone dissolved in the water. Look for the banded tufa at the base of the streaming jets.

The narrow gorge, with its sides flaring up into the sky and the double waterfall racing in spate over its tufa base, is a great climax to the walk. Return to Malham by the road or back along the pleasant riverside walk.

Falls on Cosh Beck

13

2. Waterfalls on Cosh Beck

MR 863779, $5^{1}/_{2}$ miles

PARK IN THE small hamlet of Halton Gill. There is a convenient lay-by, close to the village green, to the left of the narrow road leading from the village to Foxup. Stroll through the lanes and alleys of Halton Gill, past houses and barns built in the seventeenth century. Notice the white-topped waterfall on Halton Gill Beck descending with great haste through the snow-covered slopes of Horse Head Moor.

Follow the signpost directions for Settle, walking a short distance along the walled moorland road to Halton Gill Bridge. Pass through the signposted and gated stile on the right, on the far side of the bridge. This leads to the snowy pastures beside the surging beck. Here a heron probes in a muddy area near a small tributary and then flies to another area, free of snow, as you approach. A dipper darts upstream and then, after settling for a few minutes, turns and flies, high above your head, downstream.

Continue along the stiled footpath, keeping close to the

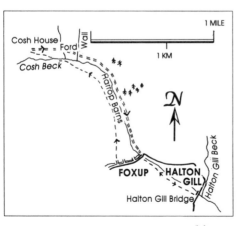

hurrying water, past many delightful falls at each drop in the bed of the tree-lined beck. Pass through a stone stile close to more lace-like cascades and then take the stile between a farmyard and the Cosh to continue along a railed path to Foxup Bridge. Look for the gaps on either side of the stone arch that allows the river

14

water through when the beck is in flood.

Turn left onto the narrow lane that gives access to the houses at Foxup. Here the OS map shows a footpath as passing through the farm, but this has been officially closed. To continue to the waterfall on Cosh Beck, and then to Cosh House, walk along the lane, passing two small stone bridges over the cascading Foxup Beck. They lead to buildings on the right. Notice the fine waterfall beneath the second bridge.

Cross the beck by the third bridge and follow a cart-track bearing to the left. Climb uphill and continue ahead along a walled track, keeping a listed barn to the left and a newly renovated house to the right.

Where the track swings left take the gap stile to the right of a gate and walk ahead to the large gap in the facing wall. Continue to the wicket gate stile, slightly to the right in the wall ahead. Here the snow is criss-crossed with the footprints of rabbits and hares. Keep the wall to the right and continue to a gap stile. From here you can hear the Cosh noisily negotiating its limestone bed.

Continue, passing a sturdy barn that lies to the right. Pass through two gated stiles and walk ahead, keeping to the left of the first of the Harrop Barns. Then pass the second barn - this one quite derelict. Pass through another gated stile and pass the last of the barns, then strike slightly uphill to the left to a stile close to a solitary ash.

Continue over the snow-covered slopes. Look ahead to the derelict building of Cosh Head - the point where the return journey starts. Follow the indistinct path downhill towards the beck. On the opposite slope a well-constructed wall drops steeply to the hurrying water. Here the lively stream descends in a glorious waterfall - the reward for the somewhat arduous walk through the snow-covered pastures. Cosh Beck thunders over shallow ledges before being forced over a lip of rock between two huge boulders. Then it cascades over ledge after ledge, foam-topped and in a haze of spray, into a very deep, dark seething pool.

Keeping beside the wall, stride upstream past more pretty cascades. Beside the next series of falls, pass through a gated stile. This gives access to the side of the moorland stream. Cross

". . one window intact"

the beck on convenient boulders, climb the slopes and walk up to Cosh House. Here the Elizabethan farmhouse is a dangerous ruin, with one lovely window intact. Beside it stands a renovated house.

Turn right in front of the buildings and pass through the gate. Continue along the high level cart-track with grand views of the snowy slopes. The Cosh is now hidden in a fold in the fells. To the left is a plantation of young conifers. Walk along the track, crossing a wide, shallow ford. Stride out, downhill. On the high slopes, where the snow has melted in the warm sunshine, dozens of sheep feed on the exposed yellowed grass.

Follow the path as it comes close to a second plantation of mixed conifers and then, where it swings towards the beck, look down to the splendid falls below a clump of ash trees. From now on the beck descends in many more charming falls which swirl and foam over its limestone bed. Continue past another plantation and walk on. Away to the right are the Harrop Barns passed earlier. Step out past a ford and then beside a deep gully in the limestone plates where the beck races through a miniature strid.

Just before Foxup look for the small, arched, cobbled bridge over the beck, just wide enough for a tractor. Below, the waters flow through a deep channel, roaring and raging as they go, shadowed by ash in swelling black bud. Walk on towards the small settlement, passing through a gate onto a walled track to the road. Turn right and take the footpath on the left, on the far side of the bridge. Retrace the footpath taken earlier.

Valley of Desolation

3. Waterfalls in Valley of Desolation, Wharfedale

MR 077556 - 082569, 3 miles

A LONG REINFORCED road leads down to the car park by Wooden Bridge over the River Wharfe. It leaves the B6160 by the Cavendish Memorial close to the remains of Bolton Priory. In late January the walker has a striking view of the ruins through leafless trees which in summer screen it from sight. Parking is expensive, but the park is close to the surging river, where dozens of mallards have already paired and where the males are aggressive. A cafe provides a good cup of tea, and there are excellent toilets.

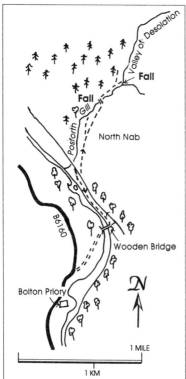

Cross the bridge, below which more mallards preen on rocks and a dipper, resplendently clad in white bib and chestnut band, bobs and runs into the fast-flowing water. Walk on to the crossroads and turn left, walking uphill past young sycamores with fat green buds, hazel bushes supporting slim long catkins gently swaying in the breeze and rose bushes still covered with fat, glossily-red, hips. The narrow lane climbs sharply, giving inviting glimpses of the Wharfe swirling round small islands far below. On the steep slope to the river grow many lofty beech trees which have carpeted the ground

18

with a thick layer of bronze leaves. Through these emerge dog's mercury laden with small green flowers.

At the top of the hill pass through a gate beside a cottage. Snowdrops, very white in the thin winter sunshine, grow in profusion in the garden. Walk straight ahead across a field to a kissing gate on the far side and continue along a wide stony track that swings out over the moorland of Posforth Gill. Regularly spaced along the path are many oak trees planted in the early eighties but still protected by wire mesh from sheep, deer and rabbits. Up on the slopes of North Nab the flash of the white scut of a rabbit confirms the need for the meshing.

Where the track divides follow the narrow path to the left down through grassy hummocks of ground to the edge of the beck. The ground on both sides of the tumbling stream slopes steeply and is covered with bracken, a glorious rich red in the bright sun. Walk upstream to the foot of the first waterfall. Here, over huge, casually littered boulders the beck leaps exultantly in two wide, roaring jets streaked with brown and falls into a broad peat-stained pool. Above the beck has broken through the middle part of a semi-circle of layered limestone, in the crevices of which grow ferns and reeds. Oak and birch lean over this secluded hollow and close to these trees flourish holly and ivy, opportunists that use the light for growth when the larger trees have lost their leaves. To the right of the fall a landslip has been planted with alders and these now carry plump golden catkins.

If the beck is in spate, making crossing difficult, return to the main path and walk along the rim of the

Dog's mercury with small green flowers

small ravine where more sturdy oaks grow. From here the waterfall is seen again together with the five small fingers of water into which the stream divides before making its spectacular jump. Continue uphill, following the path that circumvents the landslip and then, where the path divides, bear left down a steepish slope to a plank bridge across the hurrying beck. The path continues beyond the bridge into the Valley of Desolation.

The air is still. The path keeps close to the cheery sounding water. The grass is green and where tiny rivulets join the main stream there are bright green flushes full of saxifrage. A brightly coloured pheasant in full breeding plumage flies upstream. A dipper calls from a rock. It bobs and bobs and then follows the pheasant, keeping just above the dancing water. The sun comes out and the sky has small blue patches. Today the Valley of Desolation seems a quiet, hidden valley of peace and shelter - that is, until the walker looks at the trees. These are mainly oak and all of them are stunted, twisted, riven, gnarled, blasted. When a furious wind blows through the valley this must be a truly desolate, inhospitable place.

Where the path divides keep to the lower branch that leads to the bottom of the second waterfall. Here Sheepshaw Beck comes raging out of the coniferous plantation and falls in long white plumes of water on either side of a huge, wide boulder. Between the two falls a rocky island supports a young beech that grows tall and straight. Holly covered with glossy leaves grows beneath oaks and more oaks shadow the surging pool beneath the foaming frothing falls. Above the waterfall the conifer trees form a V-shaped frame that stretches into the distance where the tree-lined land slopes down to the beck. As the beck flows out of the pool it is joined by the water of Dicken Dike.

Return through the Valley, and Posforth Gill, to the lane beyond the cottage and turn right. At the bottom of the hill turn acute left onto a reinforced path that runs down to the side of the Wharfe. Follow the path through the trees to where it comes close to the islands seen earlier. Here the way has been reinforced, enabling the walker to continue dry-shod. Take the stile and walk down the steps and lean over the railed area to view the rapids below. The Wharfe flows fast and deep here and as it rejoins the water from the other side of the islands small whirlpools and eddies are created. Continue along the riverside path to the Wooden Bridge and the car park.

Twisted, riven, gnarled, blasted oaks

Pen-y-ghent Beck

4. Waterfall on Pen-y-ghent Beck, Littondale
MR 893746, 6 miles

LEAVE HALTON GILL by the signposted moorland road to Settle. After a mile park on the grass verge to the right of the first cattle-grid (not marked on the OS map). Walk on a fifth of a mile along the high level, narrow road until you reach a stile on the left, leading to a footpath, signposted Nether Hesleden. Follow the footpath as it keeps close to a wire fence. It drops steadily and easily down the steep slopes, with Pen-y-ghent Gill to the right and much limestone scar to the left.

Look across to the limekiln on the far side of the valley; just below, deep in the narrow gill, lies a double waterfall. Here the beck descends in a graceful veil of white-topped water beneath leafless trees. There is no right of way to the fall but its glory can

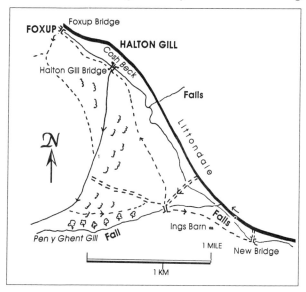

be viewed from the path.

Continue dropping downhill past more limestone outcrops. Here stunted crag-fast ash cling close to the rock to avoid the fierce winds. Just before the ladder stile look right to several stately beech still loaded with mast; and beyond, down into the gill, to another grand fall.

Walk along the track, beyond the stile, as it descends to the farm. Pass through a metal gate and walk in front of the farmhouse, built in 1748. Cross diagonally right to a gate and follow the signpost directions for Litton. Walk over the moss-covered bridge, turn left and walk across the pasture to a ladder stile. Now the Pen-y-ghent Beck flows noisily to your left, on its way to join the water from the Cosh and the Foxup and to become the River Skirfare.

Continue along the stiled way through lovely Littondale. Just before New Ings Barn, step left to view a pretty fall on the beck. After a series of rapids the fast-moving water falls in a skirt of white foam. Tiny drops of water sparkle in the morning sunshine and then all the light and sparkle disappear into a deep dark dub where the water surges against the restraining rock banks of the river.

When you can drag yourself away from this lovely fall head for the ladder stile that gives access to a short walled track, leading to the barns. Notice the stone drinking trough at the side of the track. Continue across a pasture, moving away from the beck, to more of the walled track which ends in another ladder stile.

Stride on, keeping the wall to the left, through this glorious valley. Flocks of fieldfare feed in the pastures and move off when disturbed, noisily calling to each other -

The ladder stile and New Ings Barn

24

revealing clearly the dark bands on their tails, the pale patch above their tails and their pale grey heads.

The footpath now edges back towards the river, this time the Skirfare. Just before you reach New Bridge look for the foaming cascades below. Cross the bridge and continue along the short farm track to the lane. Turn left to walk towards Halton Gill. Look left for a good view of Pen-y-ghent between Plover Hill and Darnbrook Fell. The lane keeps beside the Skirfare, where dippers call quietly, each from its chosen boulder. They hurry into the fast-flowing water, which breaks in rapids over underlying plates of limestone.

Walk on past the confluence of the Skirfare and the Pen-y-ghent, with delightful falls above and below the meeting of the waters. Further upstream, just before Cosh Beck makes a wide loop, look for another elegant fall where, in a flurry of dancing spray, the water descends to continue its urgent race to join with the Skirfare. Here, on wooded banks, hazel trees carry short, tight catkins and blue tits call from bare branches.

Turn left into the access track to Nether Hesleden Farm and follow it as it swings up the slope before the farmhouse to the farm's outbuildings. Pass through a gate and another directly ahead and follow the footpath sign, diagonally right, across the meadows towards Halton Gill. Look left from the stiled path to the ancient settlement and field system on the slopes above, where the low winter sun picks out the lines and furrows. Pass several sturdy barns before coming close to Cosh Beck.

Pass through the gated stile onto Halton Gill Bridge and through another to the pastures beyond. Follow the stiled way across the pastures to Foxup where a heron, seen on an earlier walk, still feeds. Turn left at Foxup Bridge and walk the few yards to a footpath, signposted Horton-in-Ribblesdale. Pass through an arrowed gate and climb diagonally right, following a grassy track, to a signpost by the wall.

At the three-armed signpost, do not pass through the gap in the wall but bear away to the left, moving away from the wall to a gate in the wall ahead. There is a pleasing view from here of Foxup Farm in its wooded hollow, of Halton Gill and of the U-shaped Littondale stretching into the misty distance.

Stride out along the wide grassy path across the lower skirts of Plover Hill. Pass through the next gate and follow the track as it swings to the right and rapidly comes to the cattle-grid where you have parked.

A heron feeds

Fall by Water Fall Rock

27

5. Circular walk from Long Preston, including the waterfall by Water Fall Rock
MR 855581, 6 or 8 miles

PARK IN Long Preston on the A65. If you approach from the west, you will find spaces close to the village shop and the Boar's Head Hotel, on the right side of the road. Cross the road and walk on to take the first left turn, Church Lane. Ahead is a splendid view of St Mary the Virgin. Pass through the lych gate and enter the church to enjoy its peace and tranquillity.

Leave by the lych gate and follow Church Lane round to the right. Take a turning on the right, where the ways divide, and continue keeping the churchyard wall to the right, to New House Lane. Stride along the walled lane, now, in February, under four inches of crisp snow. Follow the track downhill and cross Holme Bridge over Long Preston Beck. It chatters merrily over its rocky bed, each boulder with its cap of snow, and the gently sloping banks heavily blanketed in white.

A crow courts another in a horse-chestnut tree and several rooks call noisily from a clump of trees beside Fern Hill Farm. Walk between the dwellings at New House. Pass through a gate onto pasture and then continue uphill to a walled track to Little Newton. Here snow clothes every branch and twig of ash and sycamore that cluster about the buildings.

Pass through a series of gates and follow the footpath signs that direct you over a pleasing dry stone bridge crossing Newton Beck. And then walk uphill into Newton Gill, keeping the thinly frozen beck to your left. Where the path divides, take the lower path. Here a snipe rises from a muddy shallow of the beck and heads upstream with fast, direct flight.

Follow a narrow path beside the hurrying water to come upon

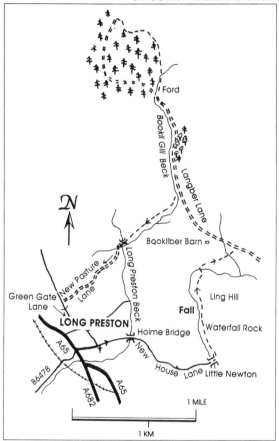

the small waterfall, tumbling in a series of foam-topped cascades below ash trees draped in white. Above the pretty fall, and the ash, stands Water Fall Rock. This large layered mass, supporting a deep shawl of snow, is composed of layers of gritstone separated by wide bands of grey shale. The gritstone catches the wintry sunshine, providing a yellow glow, the only touch of warmth in the white world of Newton Moor.

Continue beside the beck to a facing wall and then climb the slope to a stile over the wall. Beyond, the way climbs the gentle slope, the skirt of Ling Hill, veering slightly to the right, following the curve of the meandering beck that lies below. Just before a

29

Church of St Mary the Virgin

wall ahead descend the slope to climb a stile to a footbridge over the beck. Walk up the snowy bank beyond, keeping beside the wall on your right, to a gated stile.

Strike diagonally right across the gently rising pasture to a ladder stile to Langber Lane, a very wide walled drove road. Turn left and step out - as well as the snow will allow you - past Bookilber Barn. Look left to see a glorious patchwork of walled pastures, all with a varying degree of whiteness. Beyond lie glacial mounds, they too, under deep snow.

The track soon comes close to the Bookil Gill Beck. Notice, on the left, a footpath several feet below the track, signposted Long Preston. This is the return route, but if you wish to extend your walk continue on past a sturdy embankment that confines the exuberant stream. Follow the track past a small woodland of Scots pine and alders, maintained by the Woodland Trust. A notice on the gate invites visitors to walk among the trees.

Continue along the track where, over to the left, a kestrel hovers above the snowy slopes. Follow the track downhill to cross a narrow, shallow ford and the beginning of a huge plantation of conifers called Wild Share, owned by the Economic Forestry Group. At the end of the plantation, climb the stile on the left and walk the forest road, a wide smooth track of untrodden snow.

As you move into the forest small tracks appear where rabbits and birds have crossed. Larger tracks reveal the hidden presence of several deer and a fox. Intriguing feathery lines show that a swooping kestrel, perhaps the bird seen earlier, has pounced on a rodent, too lightly to leave other tracks behind.

Turn left into a wide ride and follow a thin path between rough tussocky pasture. Snow sits delicately on every branch of the bordering conifers, turning the forest into a fairyland. An overwintering meadow pipit hops between the stems of last year's seed heads, protruding from the snow-covered mounds of grass. It uses its tail as a prop as it reaches up to pass each seeded stem through its thin pointed beak. The ride continues and takes you back to Langber Lane by the ford crossed earlier.

Walk back along the lane to the signpost noted before. Leave the track and descend to the signposted gate on the right. Beyond, cross the beck on convenient stones and continue onwards. The way continues, climbing steadily above the beck, which descends through the gill in several attractive falls. Pass through a gap in the wall ahead and walk parallel with the tree-lined beck, from which comes the eerie call of a sparrowhawk. Beyond a gate in the wall ahead, walk slightly to the left to another stiled gate in a facing wall.

Follow the way as it drops steadily to a stile and a gate. Beyond, cross a narrow footbridge over Long Preston Beck. Step out along the cart-track to cross a dry stone bridge and continue uphill to a gate beside another Woodland Trust copse. You are now at the start of the walled New Pasture Lane. Stride along the track until reaching Green Gate Lane. Turn left and walk downhill to Long Preston. Turn left along the main road to reach the parking area.

The Strid

6. The Strid, Bolton Abbey, Wharfedale

MR 064565, 3¹/₂ miles

A STRONG WIND from the west encourages the walker to seek shelter. The paths on either side of the Wharfe, leading to The Strid, are protected by mature woodland and seem an excellent choice for a blustery Valentine's Day. Park as for the walk to the waterfalls in Posforth Gill (number three) and continue upstream, following the route of the Dales Way and the green marker trail through Strid Wood. This high level route gives excellent views through beech and oak to the surging deep brown Wharfe below. Beech mast lies scattered over the path and bramble, bracken, moss and a deep layer of bronze leaves litter the woodland floor. Soon, white-topped rapids replace the calm

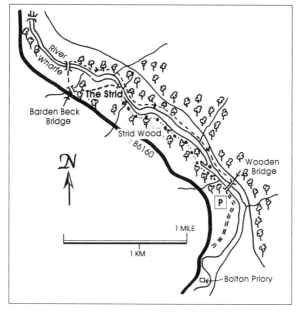

water of the stately river, divided here by six densely wooded islands.

Beyond the rapids the river flows strongly and quietly and the loud boyish whistles of nuthatches fill the air. High overhead several of these brightly coloured birds busily attack the lichen that closely adheres to the sturdy branches of tall oaks. They pivot on their legs, heads deep in the lichen and tails skywards, levering the foliage protecting overwintering insects. Bits of vegetation continually rain downwards and some quite large prey are rapidly devoured. A great spotted woodpecker flies overhead, its stiff feathered tail giving it a 'stubby' appearance.

The path continues parallel with the Wharfe, passing through beech, oak, ash and sycamore. Nearer the water hazel and alder support a mass of catkins, to the delight of a mixed flock of tits which moves rapidly through the bushes calling quietly to each other. A host of long-tailed tits passes through the tree-tops, the birds advertising their presence with constant thin calls. And then the river drowns all bird song as the waters of the Wharfe foam and roar angrily for a hundred yards through a deep incision, in some places barely six

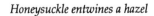

Honeysuckle entwines a hazel

34

feet wide, in the limestone rock. The banks are deeply undercut. The Strid, dangerously misleadingly named, should not be crossed. Many have tried and some have lost their lives.

Follow the path as it slopes upwards - some clambering is required here - to limestone steps beneath a tall layered rock formation. Honeysuckle, covered with fresh green leaves, entwines a hazel and more nuthatches call from the branches of an oak. Below, the dark surging water once more passes through a narrow channel in the limestone, a 'second Strid'. It is as challenging as the first, and just as dangerous. Crossing it should be left to a pair of dippers that regularly fly over the white-topped water and seem very interested in a hole in the river bank. The path leads to a wooden bridge over Barden Beck, which hurries below eager to add its deeply peat-stained water to the Wharfe. Beyond the bridge a stile on the edge of the wood gives access to parkland.

Walk on along the path, which leads to a stone, turreted footbridge over the broad gracious river. The bridge, wide enough for a haycart, has recesses at regular intervals large enough for a man to stand in. Once across the folly-type bridge turn right and return along the east bank. Parkland soon gives way to a stile into woodland, and more nuthatches. As the path climbs above the river a dipper can be seen below assiduously preening after a prolonged foray for food and there is a splendid view looking down on the 'second Strid'.

Take the first narrow path leading down to the edge of the Wharfe and carefully negotiate the huge slabs of limestone that border the Strid. Follow the path as it winds through huge oaks, past extensive plantings of young oaks snugly housed in their biodegradable casings and over mossy rocks at the very edge of the racing water. At regular intervals along the river banks pairs of mallards snooze in the mild midday air, but they are not too sleepy to guard their own reach of the Wharfe from all comers. One pair has chosen a territory close to a large patch of snowdrops.

Keep to the path as it passes the islands and climbs, via a stile, above the rapids and then crosses a meadow to the Wooden Bridge. Beyond lie the car park and dozens of mallards preening on the bank.

Falls on Park Gill Beck

7. Circular Walk from Kettlewell via the waterfalls on Park Gill Beck and Caseker Gill Beck

MR 987753 - 985744, 6 miles

FROM THE PUBLIC car park in the village of Kettlewell, turn left to cross the bridge over the Kettlewell Beck. Take the right turn, signposted Coverdale, in front of the Bluebell Hotel. Pass between the brownstone houses, keeping the chattering beck to the right. At the junction, cross the road and continue, following the signposted road to Leyburn (gradient 1 in 4). Climb the steep walled road and, where it makes a sharp right turn, continue

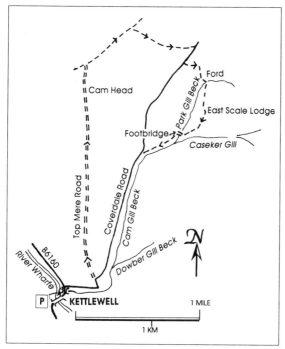

ahead along a wide walled drove road. This is called Top Mere Road on the OS map and now, in February, is deep in snow. The signpost at the start of the track says that it is one and a half miles to Cam Head.

Continue the long, steady climb, pausing to look back on Kettlewell, each roof laden with snow. Notice how the dark boundary walls contrast sharply with the snow, revealing a pleasing field pattern around the village. Pass through a gate and continue on to where the snow, trapped in the track, reaches the top of the walls. Fortunately walkers have passed this way earlier and trodden a path over the hard packed snow.

At the next gate, a small step is all that is needed to cross the top bar. Beyond, follow the track out onto Cam Head, a wild white wilderness dotted with rabbit tracks. Where the snow lies less deeply, patches of grass begin to appear from beneath the white blanket. At the signpost follow the directions for Hunters Sleet. Continue ahead keeping the wall to the right.

Pass over the next gap stile, with just a step from one snowy mound to the next. Look right to see Wharfedale stretching away into the distance with Kilnsey Crag, dark and formidable against the white valley. Walk on, following the track - which now swings left, away from the wall - until you reach the fell road. Here skiers descend the slopes.

Turn right, cross the cattle-grid and walk downhill until you reach an unmarked gate at the bottom of a steep slope, on the left, by a sheep pen. Follow the track beyond as it swings left towards the boundary wall. Continue downhill to pass through a stiled gate in the wall ahead. Stride downhill, following the track as it swings first right and then left to a ford over Park Gill Beck. Enjoy the numerous falls on this tempestuous stream. It tumbles over a series of ledges in its bed with a flurry of foam, quite grey against its snowy banks.

Beyond the ford follow the track to the right. One of the numerous rabbits tries to climb a steep snowy slope and slides back, ending facing in the opposite direction. Climb the track to East Scale Lodge, a derelict farmhouse. Pass through a gate beside a barn and turn right to pass through another. Walk ahead, keeping beside the wall on the right and pass through a gateless gap on the right.

Continue onwards along a track that begins to drop downhill. Follow it as it swings to the left at the bottom of the slope. Ahead lies a fence along the edge of the very steep slopes of Caseker Gill. Here look right to a small stile in the corner of the wall. Beyond, with care, descend the very steep slope to the footbridge over Park Gill Beck.

Look up Caseker Gill to where the beck drops in a series of sparkling cascades through confining limestone walls, beneath rowan, elm and ash. It dances over its rocky bed to descend in a small elegant fall before adding its water to the Park Gill Beck. The latter tumbles in a lace-like cascade. This is a lovely hollow.

Cross the bridge and turn left to walk parallel with the beck. Follow the path as it climbs uphill to a stile and continue beyond. Look down to the beck where it descends once more in a skirt of foaming water. Join the Coverdale road, using the ladder stile over the wall. Turn left and walk downhill to Kettlewell.

*Caseker Gill . . . adding its water
to the Park Gill Beck*

Waterfalls in Tongue Gill

8. Circular walk from Stainforth to visit Catrigg Force and the waterfalls in Tongue Gill

MR 833671 - 828676, 4½ miles

A FTER THE HEAVY snowfalls of early March, the temperature sometimes rises and torrential rain follows. Suitably clad, and prepared for getting thoroughly wet, you can now see Yorkshire's waterfalls at their most magnificent.

Park in the car park on the outskirts of the delightful village of Stainforth, with its sturdy houses clustered around the parish church and the graceful Stainforth Beck. Turn right out of the parking area and follow the road as it swings right to cross the beck. Take the narrow squeeze stile on the left, on the far side of the bridge. Walk beside the raging torrent to pass between dwellings to a small village green. This lies to the east of the stepping-stones, which give access to another small green on the

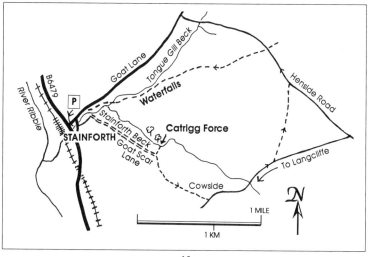

41

opposite bank. Today the stones are submerged and the turbulent waters rage over the row of boulders that would normally hinder their progress.

Walk along the road beside the green to its end and begin to ascend the rough track (Goat Lane) that continues where the tarmac ceases. Steep at first, the walled lane climbs steadily and pleasantly, giving ever-widening views of the fells. Immediately before the gate at the end of the lane, climb the stile on the left, signposted Catrigg Force.

Stroll down the slope and take the wooden stile on the left into glorious beech woodland. From here a muddy, steeply sloping path, followed by railed, stone steps (often extremely slippery), leads to the foot of a ravine and the bottom of the spectacular fall. Here the Stainforth, swollen with snow-melt and hours of continuous rain, roars over a lip into an immense hollow. It plummets in two majestic walls of white foam, one after the other, into a boiling basin. The angry river surges on, foaming, spraying, raging, to descend another steep drop in the bed of the river.

Return to the lane, and cross the ladder stile on the right and climb the slope to the right to a gate and stile. From here there is a good view of Smearsett, Ingleborough, Pen-y-ghent and Fountains Fell. Beyond, turn half-left to follow a cart-track. Pass through a gate and walk onwards, passing limestone outcrops on either side. Where the track forks take the left branch, keeping a wall to the left. Pass a limekiln on the right and walk on to the narrow moorland road. Turn left, cross the cattle-grid and walk downhill, passing beneath a glorious row of lofty horse-chestnut and beech trees.

Pass the farmhouse at Cowside, where snowdrops border the roadside, and walk on to cross the small bridge over Cowside Beck - another angry torrent. Step out along the road to the second clump of trees. Pass through the gate opposite, on the left. Here in moorland pastures meadow pipits flit from one tuft of grass to another but as yet have not started their nuptial flights. Walk ahead to take a ladder stile over the wall. Continue diagonally right from one ladder stile to the next until you reach the gate onto Henside Road.

Turn left and walk along the lonely narrow road to the

signpost on the left, pointing the way, left, to Stainforth, one and three-quarter miles. Strike diagonally right, to cross Great Catrigg Pasture, to the wall ahead. Beyond the ladder stile walk ahead along the stiled way until you reach two ladder stiles. Take the one to the right and continue once more along the stiled way until you climb the last stile before the waterfalls in Tongue Gill.

Walk to the right to see the top of the delightful fall beneath mature beech, ash and elm. At first the beck surges over a series of small drops in its bed, the water creamy white and heavily stained with peat. Then it makes its dramatic, angry descent into the sheer-sided gill in one wide sheet of roaring water. Move carefully down-stream, behind the derelict wall, to see the full glory of this furious overfull mountain stream channelled between the steep confining sides.

Continue downhill, along the path, keeping parallel to the beck, which is hidden deep in the

'... another beck descends, almost perpendicularly'

43

gill. At the bottom of the slope another beck descends, almost perpendicularly, through trees on the far bank, in a huge white cascade, to add its water to Tongue Gill Beck.

Walk along the track to pass in front of a barn to a bridge over the beck, just before it adds its swollen waters to Stainforth Beck, flowing in from the left. At the confluence white water piles on white water, creating whirlpools, turbulence and a great roaring. Climb the track as it moves up a slope from where there is a dramatic view of both becks. Follow the track as it drops to a wide grassy area where the river flows in a gracious curve. Here a foaming, brilliantly white fall races down the steep slope, like spilt cream, to tumble into the Stainforth. Strike along the track as it climbs uphill to Goat Lane. Turn left to walk downhill, past the west side of the stepping-stones, past the church and to the car park.

Hindlethwaite Gill

9. *Waterfall in Hindlethwaite Gill, Coverdale*

MR 057809, 5¹/₂ miles

C OVERDALE, ONE OF the least known of the Yorkshire Dales, lies south of West Witton and north-east of Kettlewell. The village of Horsehouse, at the start of the walk, lies on the once strategic route linking the castles of Lancaster, Skipton and Middleham. Traders and pack-horses used to pass through the dale when it was a vast deer park. Coach horses were changed at Horsehouse, where the inn refreshed the travellers.

Today the village is approached by narrow roads, some steep and twisting. The houses of the small hamlet huddle round the inn - the Thwaites Arms - and the church of St Botolph's. Visit the latter to see its magnificent weeping beech.

It is often difficult to find where to start a walk, as here. Stand

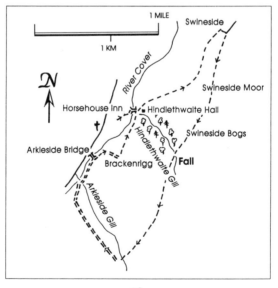

'Cross the bridge ... to Hindlethwaite Hall'

with your back to the front door of the inn, turn right and then turn right again at the end of the building. Walk left along a track, passing in front of a row of cottages. After a few yards, and just before the farm, turn right to drop down a muddy track to a signposted waymarked gate.

Pass through and walk diagonally left to a gate in the field boundary. Cross the next pasture to two gates to the right of a field barn. Pass through the gate on the right and follow the river, lined with sycamore, upstream to the narrow, gated footbridge over the hurrying River Cover. Pause here to see roe deer hinds grazing in the pastures. They stay for a few minutes and then bound off into the trees with just their white rumps visible for a second longer.

Cross the bridge and continue ahead to the front of Hindlethwaite Hall, built in the seventeenth century but extensively restored early in this. Here turn left and walk a few yards along the access track. Then strike right to the far corner of the pasture to a squeeze gap in a small piece of wall. Continue ahead, but bearing slightly right to another small piece of wall to pass through another squeeze stile.

Follow the indistinct footpath, keeping in the same general direction, to climb over two ladder stiles and to pass through a

47

gate. Continue, bearing slightly to the right, to another ladder stile. Here, in the pasture beyond, peewits frenziedly wheel and dive as we disturb them.

Continue in the same general direction (east-north-east) diagonally across the field, to a narrow gap stile just before the end of the wall. Beyond, the path continues more clearly, to pass through a gateless gap in the wall. Walk ahead, keeping to the right of a cart-track, to pass through several squeeze stiles. From here the small moorland hamlet of Swineside comes into view.

Climb a stile to the right of a gate to pass in front of the farm and continue to a tarmac road which links the cluster of dwellings, one of which is a hotel, with West Scrafton. Turn right, and where the road turns sharp left, strike right over Swineside Moor in the direction indicated by the signpost.

Step out along the rutted track as it bears left. Pass first through a line of fence posts and then grass-covered mounds, keeping the fell wall to the right. Here a pair of golden plover flies up and passes high overhead, giving a haunting fluted call. Meadow pipits hurry between clumps of rushes. Away to the left lies the rounded back of Middle Rigg.

Continue along the way, passing a barn with a blue door on your right, and the fell wall continuing. The path goes through another row of fence posts. Walk on, now with a wire fence to the right. Ahead on the skyline lies Hindlethwaite Plantation. The track swings to the left to pass to the left of a long stretch of protruding fell wall, passing through Swineside Bogs. It comes to the head of the Hindlethwaite Gill, which is clothed on both sides with larch, birch and ash.

Here, at the start of the trees, the small moorland stream hurries, white-topped between banks of bleached grass before descending a lip into the steep-sided ravine. It falls, in long strands of icy water, forming a curtain of water, into a rock-strewn pool far below. From here it rages on in numerous cascades to be lost from sight in this dramatic canyon.

Descend the gill slopes to step across the stream and climb up the other side to a good path. Walk on, keeping the fell wall to your right. Look right for an extensive view of Coverdale and of the village of Horsehouse. Follow the narrow path as it swings left, away from the wall and in line with a gap in the hills ahead - Little Whernside and Dead Man's Hill.

Continue, bearing slightly left, to pass through a gate in the fence ahead. Continue forward, passing through two more gated fences to the edge of Arkleside Gill. Drop down the slope, cross the narrow, fast-flowing stream on convenient boulders and climb up the other side to a stile beside a sheepfold. This gives access to a wide reinforced track - a pack-horse route between Nidderdale and Coverdale.

Turn right to stride downhill, with glorious views of lovely Coverdale ahead. Follow the track as it swings right to Arkleside in the valley bottom. Pass between the buildings - notice the original farmhouse built in 1681 and now used to over-winter ewes. Cross the tiny bridge and walk beside the River Cover. Pause beside the pleasing Arkleside Bridge and look across to the well-preserved limekiln on the other side.

Remain on the same bank of the surging river and step out along the good track below ash, sycamore and alder. Follow the track as it climbs uphill towards Brackenrigg. Once beyond the first dwelling take a footpath on the left. Follow the stiled and gated way, above the tree-lined slopes bordering the river, until you reach the path to Hindlethwaite Hall. Turn left to cross the footbridge and walk across the meadows to Horsehouse.

'Pause here to see roe deer hinds'

Ghaistrills Force

10. Walk to Ghaistrill's Force and Linton Falls

MR 993645 - 002633, 9 miles

L EAVE THE CAR at the Yorkshire Dales National Park Centre, Grassington. Turn left and walk towards the village centre. Goldfinches fly from tree to tree. Turn right into the main street, which is lined with interesting shops. It is easy to dawdle. Continue uphill and turn left into Chapel Street and walk until the narrow road turns sharply left. Here walk ahead through a farmyard, following signpost direction to Conistone.

Beyond the farmyard, a double-armed signpost gives the

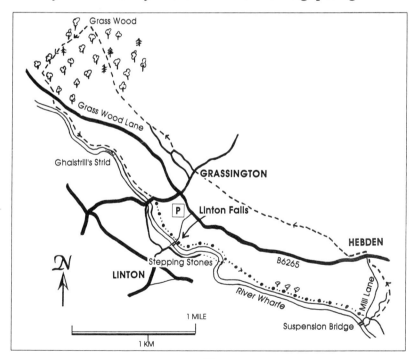

direction for Grass Wood. Pass through an exceedingly narrow gap stile and walk ahead over pastures where, in April, a scattering of ash trees still have black buds tightly closed. To the right outcrops of limestone catch the bright sun.

Look for the next gap stile in the far right-hand corner under a hawthorn covered in pale green leaf. Beyond, stone steps lead to a walled lane where celandines and milkmaids flower. Walk on to the lane end and then across a meadow to the ladder stile into Grass Wood Nature Reserve. Take the path that continues gently upwards through the lovely spring woodland. Here beneath sycamore, beech, ash, larch and Scots pine flower bluebells, dog mercury, ground ivy, pink campion and violets. A willow warbler fills the air with its wonderfully sweet song.

The path crosses the site of a prehistoric settlement and then in time passes into a small compartment of larch where goldcrests and coal-tits call. At a crossroads of paths turn left and walk a few yards to a waymarked post. Here turn right and stride over a carpet of branches used to control erosion. Walk on downhill through banks lined with primroses, bluebells and moss-covered rocks.

The path turns to the left at the wood end and passes through majestic beech trees. Below, through the trees, sparkles the River Wharfe. Turn left and walk along a footpath just before reaching Grass Wood Lane. The path ascends, passing through wood anemones. The call of a green woodpecker echoes through the trees. Look for the third narrow path on the right, which leads downhill through the trees to a small car park and Grass Wood Lane. Cross, and climb the ladder stile opposite.

Walk ahead until the stately Wharfe lies below. Turn left and follow a good path which soon drops downhill to continue beside the surging water. Then stride through trees and over greensward, where ewes suckle their lambs and cowslips grow below limestone outcrops.

Ghaistrill's Strid lies at a bend in the river. Here a deep cleft in the limestone confines the water in a narrow channel full of foam and noise. About the strid flit pied and grey wagtails. Sandpipers give their long rippling calls as they fly, restlessly, along their reach of their river. And rotund dippers sing their sweet lyrics before walking into the water after aquatic insects.

Climb the ladder stile to pass below ash. Here purple orchids and wild strawberry flower on banks. Below to the right lies Ghaistrill's Force, where the Wharfe tumbles in white-topped cascades before it becomes, once more, a wide placid stream. Here swallows wheel and dive, sweeping insects from the surface of the water.

Step out along the pleasing riverside walk and then follow the path as it swings to the left up a slope to the B6265. Cross the road to join the Dales Way, which soon swings across a wide pasture with a foaming weir away to the right. Stride on along the riverside path to the side of Linton Falls. Here the river descends in boiling foam over limestone steps, part of the North Craven Fault. Walk on to the wooden footbridge for a striking view of the racing river.

Continue on the same side of the river beyond Snake Walk and look back for a delightful view of the white-topped falls through the soft green leaves of the riverside trees. Walk on through the meadows and look across the river to the twelfth century church at Linton with its beehive bell tower.

Head on beside the Wharfe, past the stepping-stones and then across wide green pastures, where the river makes a wide bend. Follow the path as it returns once more to the riverside and pass beneath a row of grac-ious horse-chestnuts. Sandpipers fly up-stream and a mallard duck marshals ten ducklings. Soon a row

Grey wagtail, purple orchis
and wild strawberry

of elms, loaded with flowers, shades the path and the banks are lined with violets and primroses. Curlews fly overhead to the fells, giving their long liquid bubbling call. This glorious stretch of the river should be savoured slowly.

At the suspension bridge turn left before the wall and walk to the gate onto Mill Lane. Turn right, cross the bridge over the beck and take the signposted footpath to the left. Pass between the houses and then follow the footpath through meadows. A cobbled path leads to a kissing gate. Beyond, turn right and walk through the main street of the village of Hebden to its junction with the B6265. Turn left, cross the road and walk past the inn. Take the second signposted footpath to Grassington and walk along a grand walled track where celandines spangle the verges.

Continue ahead, using the well-maintained stiles. A signpost points the way over a grassy area with the disused buildings of a hospital on either side. Where the path divides take the right branch to the corner of the buildings and two more signposts to direct you on your way.

The high level way continues with more sturdy stiles and waymarks to the start of High Lane - another walled lane, pleasant in summer but muddy in winter. Follow the lane into Grassington.

Celandines

How Stean Gorge

11. A Walk in Nidderdale

MR 093735, 11 miles, 6 hours

T HE NIDDERDALE WAY is a fifty-three-mile walk round the valley of the River Nidd. It is excellently waymarked with painted posts, signposts and small arrows. The eleven-mile circular walk described below visits the waterfalls in How Stean Gorge and then follows the Way to Scar House Reservoir and back, passing two small but pretty falls on the way.

Park in the free car park in the centre of the small village of Lofthouse, seven miles from Pateley Bridge. Walk down the hill between the warm-coloured stone houses to the T-junction by Station House. Turn right, following the direction for Middlesmoor and Stean. Cross the bridge over the dry river bed and take the turning on the left. This leads to Nidderdale's famous limestone gorge, with waterfalls, cascades and caves.

Pay your admission fee and walk along the paths beside the narrow canyon. How Stean Beck, once high above your head, has cut its way deeper and deeper for thousands of years, so that now the bed of the stream lies many, many feet below.

In May walk through the dark-coloured bluebells, woodruff and wild ramsons. Listen to the glorious bird song; the wren and the willow warbler dominate all others. Above all, enjoy the foam-topped, deep-blue water racing over the limestone boulders, surging below overhang and tumbling down innumerable falls. Before you leave, and if you have hired a torch at the entrance, scramble through Tom Taylor's Cave near the first footbridge. It is 530 feet in length, quite safe, dry for most of the way and magical to walk through.

Walk back to the Middlesmoor road. Cross over and take the unmarked gap stile in the wall ahead. Follow the field path uphill, through more stiles to the church of St Chad, Middlesmoor. Enjoy the peace of this oak-pewed church, perched on the edge of the village on its 1000 feet high round hill. Outside, read some of the epitaphs on the gravestones telling you of the many childhood deaths and of the occupations of past villagers.

Sit on the bench seat and gaze on one of the most spectacular views in the Dales. Then leave the churchyard by the cobbled lane that leads into the tiny, attractive village. Turn right and walk to the road end and the first waymark. Beyond, for two miles, continues In Moor Lane, a wide, walled and sometimes rutted cart-track, which swings out over the heather moorland. Stride uphill and enjoy the extensive views down into the How Stean

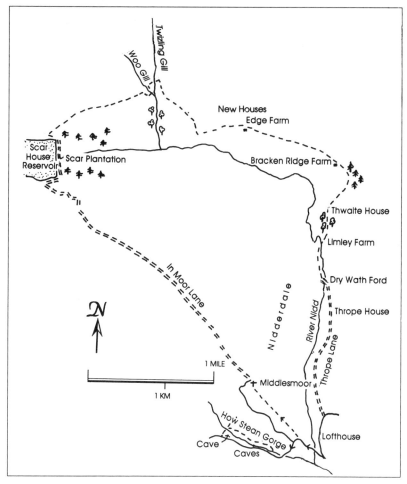

"An oyster-catcher pipes plaintively from a shingle 'beach'"

valley.

The track ends at a gate but a clear stony path continues beyond. Head along this as it first crosses the open moorland, then drops downhill in wide zig-zags. It passes below huge boulders of millstone grit as it gradually descends to the edge of the Scar House Reservoir.

Turn right beside the shoreline following the Nidderdale Way signpost. Sandpipers call from the rocky edge and an oystercatcher pipes plaintively from a shingle 'beach'. Look up the tranquil stretch of water to Great and Little Whernside and then cross the dam head. A plaque in the wall tells you that work began in 1921 and was completed in 1936. Look through the gaps between the turrets to the distant hills and peer over the other side down the immensely steep drop to the conifers of Scar Plantation.

Follow the Nidderdale waymarks beyond the dam to join a bridlepath that climbs steadily uphill to the right. The path then continues over the open moor, regularly and clearly indicated with waymarked posts. Here red grouse fly noisily into the air, soon to settle again.

Pass through the fell gate and stride along a cobbled path beside a beech plantation. Just beyond the wall take a right fork down the slope to the boundary wall. Turn left and walk on to the next gate. Beyond drop downhill. Look for the confluence of the Woo and the Twizling away to the right. Both becks are bordered with rowans and birch from where willow warblers call. A curlew flies overhead.

Cross the plank bridge and climb out of Woo Gill. The path then dips into Twizling Gill. Look for the pretty waterfall under a silver birch where sphagnum moss, heather and bilberry thrive in the spray.

Climb the track out of the gill until it fades and then continue across open fell following more waymarked posts. Here wheatears flit over last year's dead bracken, settling momentarily on the emerging green croziers. Green plovers call, hauntingly, as they wheel and dive.

Beyond the fell gate the track begins dropping steadily to the right. Look back here for your last glimpse of the reservoir. The steep track swings left and then right before levelling out to pass New Houses Edge Farm, Nidd Cottage and Bracken Ridge Farm. As the track descends to cross a small beck, look towards the conifer plantation on the left to where it makes its exit from among the trees, sparkling and gurgling as it tumbles over liverworts, moss and yellow saxifrage.

Continue along the wide track as it begins to climb uphill

'Red grouse fly noisily into the air'

towards Thwaite House. Walk a short stretch of walled track, then pass left through a gate to the lawn at the front of the house. Then take a gate to the right through to another short walled lane. Follow the waymarked track, keeping the wall to the left, into deciduous woodland. Turn right down a steep path through the trees, where bluebells, wood sorrel and violets flower. At the bottom of the slope, bear left beside a moss-covered wall. Cross the dry bed of the River Nidd (whose waters have gone underground at Goyden Pot), and walk through Limley Farm.

Follow the waymarked route beside the dry Nidd, crossing a stile on the left. Turn right beneath alders, where a pair of redstarts court, and walk downstream to another stile. Turn left and walk beside the wire fence to another ladder stile (with an astounding number of steps on the far side). Cross the dry river bed again (Dry Wath ford) and walk on into a walled lane. Continue past Thrope Farm and then follow the track called Thrope Lane. With delightful views into the valley below, the track passes through gated fields for a mile until the Masham road is reached. Turn right and walk downhill into Lofthouse.

Scaleber Force

12. Scaleber Force and Attermire Scar
MR 841626, 6½ miles

PARK IN THE car park in the north-east corner of the market town of Settle. Leave by the footpath that leads to the south-east exit, climbing uphill to a small recreation ground. Turn left and then right to ascend Albert Hill, signposted Airton. At the junction of roads by the Congregational church, take the right turn and walk past scattered buildings. Look on the left for the sturdy, dry stone enclosure once used to hold stray animals. From here there is a footpath leading uphill - but those who prefer to avoid lively heifers and a bull should continue along the walled Mitchell Lane. In June the verges are a mass of colour, with campion, bedstraw, vetch, crosswort and pink and white clover, the later most attractive to bees.

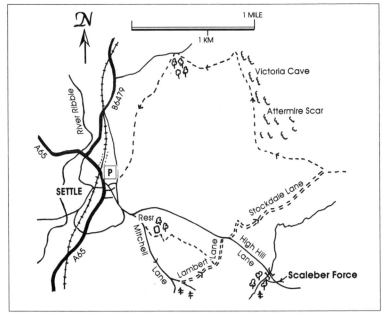

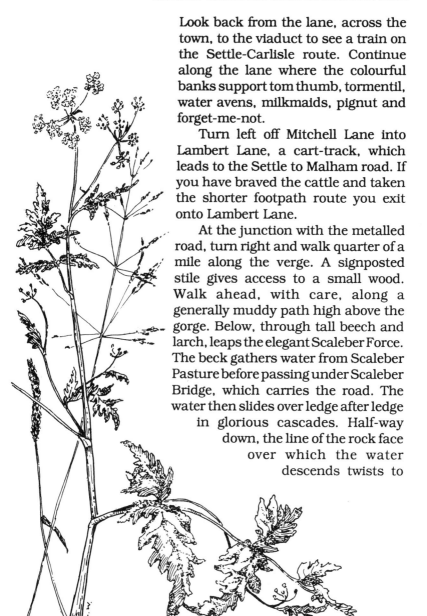

Look back from the lane, across the town, to the viaduct to see a train on the Settle-Carlisle route. Continue along the lane where the colourful banks support tom thumb, tormentil, water avens, milkmaids, pignut and forget-me-not.

Turn left off Mitchell Lane into Lambert Lane, a cart-track, which leads to the Settle to Malham road. If you have braved the cattle and taken the shorter footpath route you exit onto Lambert Lane.

At the junction with the metalled road, turn right and walk quarter of a mile along the verge. A signposted stile gives access to a small wood. Walk ahead, with care, along a generally muddy path high above the gorge. Below, through tall beech and larch, leaps the elegant Scaleber Force. The beck gathers water from Scaleber Pasture before passing under Scaleber Bridge, which carries the road. The water then slides over ledge after ledge in glorious cascades. Half-way down, the line of the rock face over which the water descends twists to

Pignut

the right and the water also veers to the right, tumbling in foaming falls into a boiling pool. The beck races on through the ravine, one small fall after another. On the steep slopes grow moss and fern and between the plants lie last year's bronzed beech leaves.

Return to the stile and beyond turn left and walk back for rather less than a quarter of a mile. Take the narrow, walled, metalled Stockdale Lane, which leads to the right. Here again colourful midsummer flowers crowd the verges. Meadow pipits serenade, rising high in the warm June air. Look for the signposted footpath to the left. The path leads below flaring limestone cliffs. In the wall to the left a stoat dances over the stones and then disappears into a hole.

Pass through a series of three gates. In a pasture beside the path a pair of green plovers call and screech as they mob a kestrel that comes too close to their nest. They dive towards the raptor and eventually send it away. Curlews call from a wet area to the south which once was a shallow lake, but has been drained to provide grazing.

Turn right before a gateless gap in the wall. Look for the cairn higher up the indistinct track indicating the way to Victoria Cave and Attermire Scar. Follow the stony track and continue where it becomes wide and grassy. Beyond a ladder stile the scar lies to the right and a wall to the left. The path becomes narrow and rock-strewn. Take a path on the right to Victoria Cave. Once this huge cavern could be entered only by a narrow slit. Now its wide

entrance - enormously enlarged during various exploratory digs - allows you to walk in. There are two side tunnels but these are dark and dangerous.

The cave was discovered by Michael Horner in 1838 while walking on the public holiday for the coronation of Queen Victoria. It has since revealed prehistoric and Roman remains. Now only jackdaws are the obvious inhabitants and a fledgling calls piteously to be fed. Among the crevices

A stoat

grow ferns, young elms and wild roses laden with blossom.

Leave the cave by a narrow path and continue along the main path between the scar and the wall until reaching a signposted ladder stile. Beyond turn left and walk down a cart-track, passing through two gates. Continue on this splendid track, where wheatears flit from limestone outcrop to wall. Overhead a pair of jackdaws harry a kestrel - perhaps the one seen earlier - as it flies off with a large morsel in its claw.

At the next gate, pass through and walk a few yards to the Langcliffe Road. Almost immediately turn left to a gate giving access to pasture beside woodland. Follow the wall round to the left to the corner of the wood. From here look north to see the stark, severe bulk of Pen-y-ghent rearing upwards. To the north-west stands Ingleborough, with its distinctive outline.

Continue along the path below a wood, then pass through a field. Step out along the edge of another wood to a ladder stile. Beyond head to the right to a gate. Pass through and continue ahead, keeping to the left of a wall. Look across to the right to Langcliffe village and its mill.

Walk ahead to a gate that leads to a wide, tree-lined track. Continue along this to the road. Turn left and walk down Constitution Hill. Where there is a fork bear left and continue until reaching Albert Hill. Take the right fork and then turn right into the children's playground and down the path to the car park.

'clover attractive to bees'

65

'. . . *over this cliff the beck once tumbled*'

13. Waterfalls at Gordale Scar and on the River Aire

MR 916641 - 899634, 7 miles

P ARK IN THE car park in the small village of Malham where a little owl, a species often seen during daylight, perches on a telegraph pole. Walk through the village and cross the bridge over Malham Beck. Continue onwards and take a left turn bordered with sweet cicely and signposted to the youth hostel. Once past the building, turn right to pass King House, the dwelling painted by John Ruskin in 1876 and entitled *Cottage at Malham.*

Continue past the old schoolhouse, turning left into Malham Rakes, a narrow, walled lane and follow it uphill and out of the village. Climb the signposted ladder stile on the right and head downhill. Pass Cawden Flats Barn, where swallows nest. Continue over pastures, where dozens of skylarks rise, singing, into the air. Look left across the intervening valley to the interesting wall patterns beside Smearbottoms Lane, which leads to Mastiles Lane.

On reaching Gordale Lane, turn left, and after visiting the old bridge, walk on to the signposted track to Gordale Scar. Follow the track beside Gordale Beck into the dark hollow at the base of the spectacular limestone cliffs. Stand and watch the house martins nesting in the hollows of the cliff, undisturbed by the roped climber nearby. As you round a corner into the gorge the waterfall lies ahead. The way continues up the bed of the fall. In winter this is often a magnificent torrent and you must expect a wet climb. In summer, and particularly after a dry spell, only a small but elegant fall drops over the tufa-covered rocks.

A sleepy little owl perches on a telegraph pole

Ascend the middle part of the fall - doing so requires some scrambling and agility - to the scree-covered hollow above. Look right to the lively waterfall descending through a hole in the rock face. This was originally blocked by natural debris.

Climb the many rock steps that lie close to the face of the gorge until you reach a plateau above. To the right, out of sight in a deep, narrow hollow, flows Gordale Beck. This was a deep, narrow lake until a violent flood in the early part of the eighteenth century washed the plug of debris from the end of the lake and sent the stream down the two waterfalls on the course it follows today.

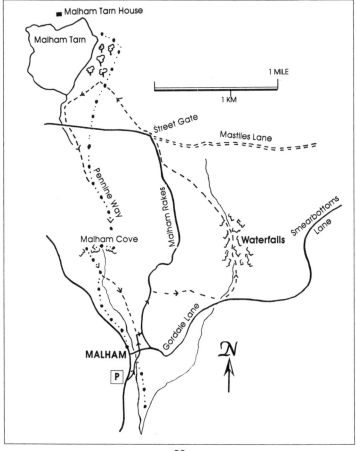

Continue along the path through a limestone wonderland. Wheatears flit across the path, unworried by the peregrine flying overhead. It utters its fierce, high-pitched scream before diving headlong out of sight. Stride on, following short waymarked posts to the throughs onto Malham Rakes. Turn right and walk along a wide track by the wall to Street Gate on Mastiles Lane, an old drove road. Turn left and at the junction with the metalled road go right to walk the dusty track towards Malham Tarn.

At the plantation turn left and walk over the moor, keeping parallel with the wall to the side of the tarn. Sit on the bank and watch and listen to the dozens of coot that keep together just off shore. Watch the sandpipers flitting from rock to rock. Look across the placid water to the field studies centre, once the fine house where Ruskin stayed when he painted his pictures of the cottage and of Gordale Scar.

Leave the tarn and walk beside the outflow stream to the road. Cross the bridge over the beck and pass through the signposted gate on the left. Keep beside the stream, where the pretty butterwort flowers in the marshy ground, to Water Sinks - which is just what the beck does. Follow the now dry river bed to join the Pennine Way. Walk on through more glorious limestone scenery, where yellow rock rose cushions ledges and forget-me-nots grow. Rose bushes laden with creamy flowers dot the slopes and wood cranesbill thrive beside the path.

At the two-armed signpost turn right and climb to the magnificent limestone pavement above Malham Cove. Look in the grikes between the

Malham forget-me-nots

clints for wood sorrel, herb robert, hart's tongue fern, aspleniun fern and dog's mercury flourishing in the shady environment. It is said that the grikes run in a south-south-east to north-north-west direction and that a walker need never be completely lost for a compass.

Walk, with care, to the far end and descend the many steps, through ash, to the base of this splendid 360 foot limestone scar to see the young River Aire appearing from the bottom. Once the beck tumbled over this cliff - what a stupendous waterfall that must have been!

Follow the young Aire on the far side as it dawdles on its way towards Malham. Pause and look

'Follow the track into the dark hollow'

back at the wonderful amphitheatre and notice how the beck has worn away the base of the huge wall of rock so that it now flares outward. Listen to the willow warblers, which sing so sweetly in the ash trees about the cove. Look for the family of wrens dotted about the boulders in the stream, all chirping at once.

Step on along the path, gradually moving away from the beck, to cross buttercup meadows. When the caravan site comes into view look for the foaming waterfall away to the right. Here the River Aire descends in white-topped glory under a clump of ash trees; alas, as it is on private ground it has to be viewed and admired from afar.

Continue along the path, passing the youth hostel, to return to the village.

Dowber Gill

71

14. Cascades in Dowber Gill and on to Great Whernside

MR 978726, 7 miles

FROM THE PUBLIC car park in Kettlewell, turn left and walk to the bridge over the Kettlewell Beck. Do not cross but walk to the other side of the road and continue along the road ahead past the public toilets, keeping the lively Cam to your left. At the next junction, where there is an interesting weather vane on a maypole in the centre of a grassy island, turn left. Walk on past the King's Head Hotel and then continue along the lane that runs along the right bank of the Cam.

Follow the lane as it turns left beside the stream and continue ahead onto a wide cart-track. Sweet cicely, already seeded in July, fills the air with its pungent smell and the abundant blue cranesbill delights the eye. Walk a hundred yards to cross the small, sturdy Dowber Bridge. Take the signposted footpath to the right on the left bank of Dowber Beck. (In summer it is obscured by a splendid ash tree.)

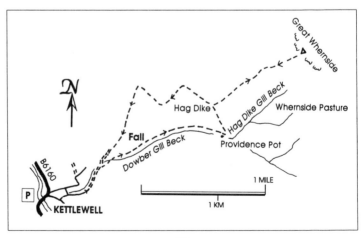

A few yards along the beck turn left through a gate, and then turn right to walk up the gill, keeping the beck to the right, following the signpost direction for Providence Pot. Aim for the ladder stile over the wall in the corner of the pasture. The Dowber dances merrily downhill beneath ash trees where goldfinches twitter.

The path, easy to follow, is bordered with eyebright, tormentil, thyme, bedstraw, milkwort, and common rock rose growing in profusion. Over this colourful display flits a small blue butterfly. Walk on to where the Dowber attractively cascades, in white-topped foam, over six wide terraces in the bedrock. Beneath each fall is a swirling brown pool. Ash, sycamore, hazel and hawthorn edge the racing water.

Continue climbing steadily through the narrowing gill, which is shadowed by steeper slopes. Where a small stream joins the Dowber on the left, beneath a large ash, the beck sinks and its bed becomes dry. The path now rises above the beck before returning to the side of the water again. It is easy to walk in dry weather, but be careful after rain.

Look for the groove running down the hillside on the left. This is probably an old 'hush' once used to expose a vein of lead. Miners would have dammed a stream at the top of the vein, then allowed the water to run down, removing the rock and uncovering the ore.

Walk on along the gill until reaching Providence Pot. The opening is surrounded with concrete and boulders in which is fitted an iron manhole. Peer through the hole in the cover to see the steps descending into the inky blackness. Between the boulders about the path flowers wild strawberry.

Look up the slopes on the opposite bank to see the Providence Lead Mine. All that remains is flat areas, once used for 'dressing' the rock to remove the precious lead. This was hard work and was done by women and children using heavy mallets to crush the rock. The ore was

Thyme and blue butterfly

then transported to the smelt mill in the valley.

Turn left and follow a narrow path, through bracken in the summer, to Hag Dike, probably once a mine building and now used by the scouts. Turn right beside the wall and climb the rough path up a steep slope to a row of cairns. From here look across to Providence Mine to see more clearly the remains of the dressing floor and a fan-shaped spoil heap. Beyond the mine look for the Whernside turf road, well-marked with posts. This would have been used to take peats, cut from Whernside Pasture above, for providing the sustained heat required for smelting.

Continue ahead along the narrow, indistinct path over Whernside Pasture, aiming for the cairn and triangulation point on the 2309 feet summit of Great Whernside, immediately above. Notice the huge outcrop of gritstone, fissured and cracked. Look in the grikes for delicate ferns. Sit on one of the enormous boulders that have split away from the parent outcrop and then tumbled sideways. On a clear day, Yorkshire stretches away in all directions. Enjoy the breathtaking views and the glorious air - and perhaps give a thought to those miners, over the centuries, who tramped Dowber Gill. Think of their hazardous struggles, under appalling conditions, to win the lead from the mine.

About the extensive top of Whernside both meadow pipits and skylarks rise into the air, singing.

Common rock rose grow in profusion

74

A pair of golden plovers flies from rock to rock, uttering its 'creaking door' call, anxious for its brood close by.

Return to Hag Dike, noticing as you descend the delicate water crowfoot flowering in the small streams that drain the pasture. Just before Hag Dike climb the wall, using the through stile. Follow the track round the building to the gate. Stride out along the track beyond as it makes two dog-leg bends to reach the valley below. Swifts scream overhead and wheatears flit about the walls. Look ahead, across the valley, to a disused mine tip and beside it, to the left, two hushes with the remains of brickwork used for damming. Pass through the gate and follow the steep track downwards. It is bounded by limestone walls. Here in the verges grows a profusion of summer flowers.

Just before Dowber Bridge look over the wall to see traces of the smelt mill. What a busy area this must once have been. Now all is quiet and peaceful but the atmosphere of days gone by still lingers.

Return to the car park.

'A pair of golden plovers fly from rock to rock

Scala Fall

15. Scala Waterfall on Hebden Beck
MR 024639, 6½ miles

PARK UNDER THE lime trees opposite the post office in the pretty brownstone village of Hebden. Green hill slopes surround this quiet corner of the Dales. Cross the B6265 and stride along the narrow lane with the beck running cheerily to the right. Soon the lane is edged with dry stone walls. Continue as far as the hamlet called Jerry and Ben's by the villagers but labelled Hole Bottom on the OS map.

After passing between the scattered dwelling, follow the

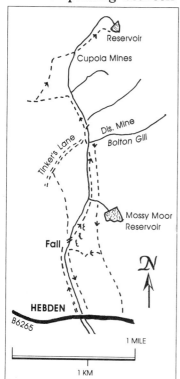

direction for the bridleway on a green signboard; this bears off right. Cross the small dry stone bridge and walk along the right side of the beck. It is lined with rowan, now in late August heavily laden with bright red berries. To the right of the path millstone grit cliffs rear upwards.

Pass through the gate and walk on. Look for a gated mine level on the right. This was probably cut in the late nineteenth century to search for lead. As you continue look for spoil heaps on the other side of the beck and, behind these, a fenced area. This was the entrance to Duke's Level and was cut in the late eighteenth and early nineteenth century.

Step out along the path past more evidence of disused buildings and more mine levels. Pass through a gate and look up right to see Bolton Gill shaft (to be visited on the return walk). Cross the beck where convenient and pass the bottom of the track called Tinker's Lane. Pass through a gate and walk on along the left side of the beck, passing over huge spoil heaps. Re-cross the small stream on boulders when the path comes to the water's edge and continue along the other side to pass through a squeeze stile.

Walk on and take a track rising through the bracken on the right. It leads up onto heather-clad moorland where grouse scold and call. Follow the track to a ladder stile and an information panel giving details of the Grassington Moor conservation area which you are about to enter. Visitors to the ruins of the Cupola smelt mines (closed in 1882) are reminded that the area is privately owned. They are requested to keep to recognised paths, not to stand too close to old shafts and not to walk in areas that are labelled dangerous on the accompanying map.

Follow the path uphill in the direction of the restored chimney. Look for the series of flues (nearly a mile in length) leading to the chimney. These controlled the temperature of the furnace. Arched entrances placed at regular intervals allowed access to boys who scraped the condensation products of white lead and arsenic from the walls. Nearer to the chimney the flues are flagged.

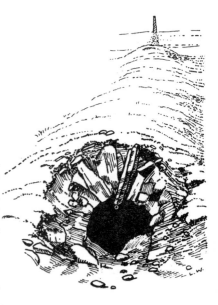

Continue ahead from the chimney to High Winding dam, which was used to provide water to power the huge water-wheel at High Winding House - only the wheel pit now remains. Walk the paths around this very interesting area of nineteenth century relics of lead mining. Each section is extremely well-labelled.

'flue, nearly a mile in length'

Return to the ladder stile, cross the heather moor and walk down through the bracken to the side of Hebden Beck. Walk back to Bolton Gill. This time walk uphill to Bolton Gill shaft, the stonework of which is excellently restored. This housed pumping gear to remove water from lower levels of the mine.

Walk back down the gill and just before reaching the beck take a path off to the left, which rises rapidly through the bracken to a gate in a wall. Walk ahead to the next gate. Beyond, stride out, and when approaching a wall directly ahead, keep to the left. Pass through the next gate and walk over to a raised bank on the left. Beyond the bank lies Mossy Moor Reservoir, which once provided water for the water-wheel at Bolton Gill mine. Today the reservoir provides a haven for migrating birds and in August it is favoured by a large flock of black backed gulls and several curlews.

Pass through a gate ahead and walk along the path through glorious banks of sweetly scented heather. This is a managed grouse moor and from August to December might be used for shooting. Obtain details of whether it is safe to walk this way from the national park office. Today only the grouse and red admiral butterflies are evident.

Where the path joins a narrow road, turn right, walking over a cattle-grid, and follow the road to a farmhouse. At a wall turn right and follow the wall round to a signposted gap. Walk down a zig-zagging path to the bottom of a steep slope. Here do not walk ahead over the flat grassy turf but turn right, keeping beside the wall on the left. This leads gently downhill through ash trees to a small gorge where the Hebden Beck descends over moss-covered millstone grit ledges. Three glorious lace-like falls tumble into a dark basin shadowed by rowan, ash, sycamore and hazel. Here a heron noisily chases a green woodpecker. The woodpecker flies to the trunk of an ash and the heron circles the tree before winging away. The woodpecker begins to climb and probe the bark of its refuge.

This is a delightful waterfall set in idyllic woodland, with the sharply contrasting austere millstone grit slopes above to the east. Walk downstream taking care along the sloping bank. Walk past a sturdy barn to a wicket gated stile. Continue diagonally across two meadows to the edge of the village. Look left to the remains of the village pinfold, once used to hold the stray animals of the village. Pass in front of the cottages and cross the small bridge over Hebden Beck. Turn left, cross the B6265 and walk to your car.

'The woodpecker climbs and probes the bark'

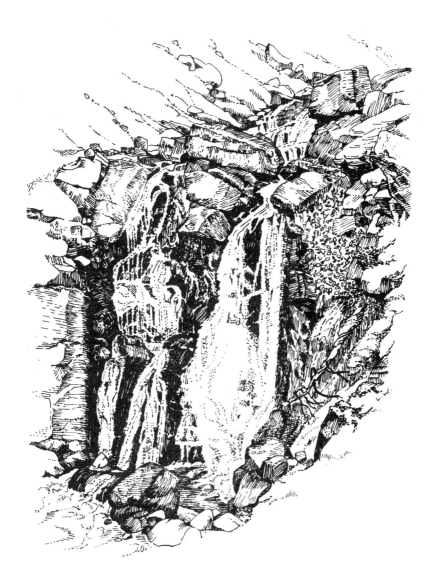

Waterfall Gill

16. Circular walk to the waterfall in Waterfall Gill from Embsay

MR 984568, 9½ miles,

PARK IN THE car park opposite the village hall at Embsay. It is not well signposted and you come upon it unexpectedly, so be prepared! Leave the car park by the signposted stile and turn right, walking diagonally over pasture to a stone stile in the corner. The narrow path continues beyond, with brownstone houses to the right and a wall to the left. Cross the next stone stile and walk diagonally to the far corner to turn left along a road, passing the church of St Mary the Virgin. Just beyond the church take the well-signposted path on the other side of the road.

Stride out along a reinforced footpath across a meadow, pass through a gate and walk on to a gate giving access to a road. Here turn left and walk a hundred yards. Turn right at a signposted bridleway, to Embsay Crag and Reservoir, just before a sharp bend in the road and a name board for Embsay. Step out along the track and the continuing farm track, which runs across lush grassy meadows.

Pass beside farm buildings and follow a bridleway signpost pointing to a ladder stile. Continue until, once beyond the fell wall, a signpost directs you left. Begin the steady ascent to Embsay Crag. In August the wide, peaty path passes through bracken but is easy to follow. Where it forks take the right branch. Look right to glorious heather moor and left to Skipton.

Climb to the top of the crag where heather, bilberry and crowberry grow. Meadow pipits flit about the millstone grit boulders. Below lies Embsay Moor Reservoir, colourful with sailing dinghies. Yorkshire lies all around.

There are several paths off the crag, all leading downhill and passing through bracken. Aim for the far side (west) of the reservoir. Where the ground is wet the path becomes indistinct but it soon re-appears. Continue to a bridge across a beck and walk to a stile that gives access to a farm road. Do not cross the stile but keep to the right of the fence. Cross a large patch of rushes and begin the ascent right, climbing towards Embsay Moor.

The way is steepish but there are many paths to choose from; all gradually merge, keeping the wall to the left. Soon the conifers of Crookrise Wood, beyond the wall, soften the hill slope, and the calls of coal tits and goldcrests can be heard. Pass between enormous boulders and beyond look for a great tumble of gritstone blocks over the wall. Another short, sharp climb brings you to the edge of the colourful heather moor, stretching away as

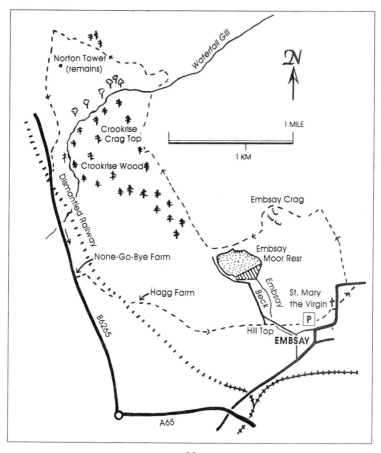

Crookrise Crag

far as you can see. Bear left and climb the ladder stile on the left.

This gives access to Crookrise Crag Top. Sit on one of the many huge crags and enjoy the wonderful view, down to the forest and away over rural Yorkshire. Walk on along the heather-covered ridge, keeping the wall to the right. This lovely path should not be missed and is a great reward for the long climb upwards. Overhead house martins scream as they dart after insects rising on the upwelling air currents.

Beyond some bonzoid Scots pine lies a triangulation point and another ladder stile. Use this to regain the lovely purple moor and walk on, keeping the wall to the left. Pass below another group of gritstone crags and continue along the moorland path, still keeping the wall to the left. Here good paths pass through low growing bracken.

Where the path branches, take the right fork, moving away from the forest. The path continues to veer steadily right through more enormous boulders. It then drops steadily down into Waterfall Gill. The waterfall, the object of this long walk, lies below. Three white-topped falls, side by side, descend dramatically into a deep, dark brown basin. A young rowan laden with vermilion berries leans over the tumbling water. A pair of grey wagtails flits about the rocks at its foot. This is a bleak, rather formidable place, but when softened with heather and bilberry it has a charm of its own.

Follow the narrow path as it continues into the gill and down to the side of the beck, where there is a small island. Step across to the island and then to the far bank. Continue walking along ill-defined tracks, upstream. Keep beside the hurrying water until you reach the first of a series of wooden frames and then strike uphill using an overgrown path. At the top of the slope, turn left onto the clear path that runs along the top of the ridge. Walk on along the edge of heather moor where grouse fly up giving their raucous 'go-back, go-back, go-back' call. On coming close to a wall follow the path round to the right, keeping the wall to the left.

After ten yards pass through a waymarked gate with a bench mark on it. Take the right-hand path and walk towards a waymarked post. A second post marks the start of a wide grassy track dropping steadily downhill. Pass through a gate and look for an indistinct footpath that passes to the left of a copse of trees. Away to the left lie the remains of Norton Tower. The path sweeps down to a signposted gate that leads to an old coach road. Turn left and walk the wide, grassy track below beech and sycamore.

The old coach road

Pass through a gate and walk on, keeping close to the wall on your right, along the route of the coach road, still discernible in places. On reaching the Grassington Road (B6265), turn left and walk three-quarters of a mile to None-go-Bye Farm. Turn left, following the signpost directions, and then right to pass Flates Barn on the left. Beyond the farm, head for the stile in the far left corner. Cross the railway track, using stiles on either side, and continue on. Follow the path to pass in front of Hagg Farm and then continue over the quiet level fields keeping to the right of the wall, all the way to Hill Top Farm.

Follow the footpath down the slope to the narrow footbridge over Embsay Beck - enjoy this quiet corner. At the road, turn right and then take a signposted footpath on the left that passes over several stiled fields to the car park.

Heugh Gill

17. A Circular Walk that includes the waterfalls in Heugh Gill

MR 018548, 6 miles

PARK IN THE car park at Embsay as for walk number 16. Turn right and cross pastures to the church. Take the field path opposite the church to the road at Eastby, as for the previous walk. At the road turn right and walk along between the houses to a left turn named Hunters Croft, signposted Eastby Moor. Bear slightly left and then walk straight ahead to a wooden stile, again signposted Eastby Moor.

Walk up the path, an old sunken sledge track, between

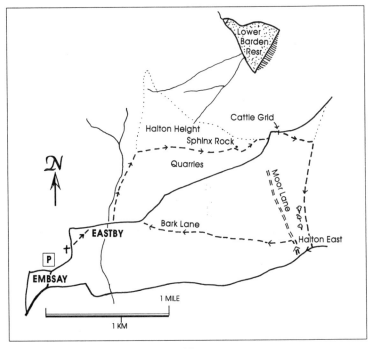

sloping banks shaded by sycamore and beech, to another wooden stile. This leads to pastures where harebells grow along the banks. Keep along the path, above two sledge tracks, close to the wall on the left. Continue over another wooden stile, quickly followed by a waymarked ladder stile. A kestrel flies overhead and then begins quartering the moor for prey.

Walk on along the path. To the left, and down a steepish slope, lies the attractive, wooded Heugh Gill. Charming cascades, in a flurry of sparkling water where the sun catches the droplets, hurry noisily downhill. The pretty, lively beck passes urgently under alder, ash, holly and sycamore. In September, bracken fronds and the leaves of the trees prevent your viewing the falls from the path above. It is possible, with care, to descend the slopes a few yards along the path and then walk back along the steep lower slopes to the cascades - but if the descent seems too difficult, then leave the viewing until after leaf fall.

From the high level path look left to Embsay Crag, visited on the last walk. Continue to a ladder stile and to the next, and to another onto Eastby Moor. Here, turn right, keeping a wall to your right and walk on along a narrow path through acres of glorious heather with a scattering of bilberry and crowberry. Look back to see Embsay Crag again and also the top of Crookrise

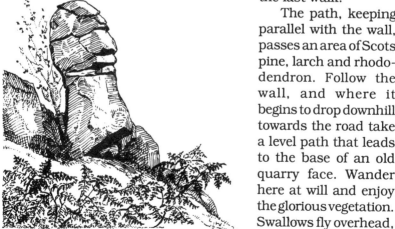

'. . . aptly named, Sphinx Rock'

Crag, also visited on the last walk.

The path, keeping parallel with the wall, passes an area of Scots pine, larch and rhododendron. Follow the wall, and where it begins to drop downhill towards the road take a level path that leads to the base of an old quarry face. Wander here at will and enjoy the glorious vegetation. Swallows fly overhead,

89

brambles

feasting on the myriad of flies in the warm air. Look over the patchwork of fields below and then continue across the quarry floor. Ascend a narrow path that leads to the base of an interesting rock formation, aptly named Sphinx rock - from the back it seems to be wearing a cap! Then continue climbing through bracken to the edge of the heather moor, Halton Height, where grouse scold and fly low over the sweetly scented heather.

As you continue, Lower Barden Reservoir comes into sight to your left. Follow narrow paths downhill to a car park (lay-by) on the Eastby road. Here turn left and walk to a cattle-grid. Beyond, on the right side of the road, take a bridleway signposted Bolton Abbey. Enjoy this springy grassy track, where mushrooms grow. Turn right off the track just before the wall and follow an indistinct path to a ladder stile over the wall ahead. Stride straight on to a stone stile and beyond cross diagonally right to another stone stile in the far corner. Here a bull grazes among its cows.

Walk on keeping a wall to your right. Beyond grows a small wood. Pass through a gate and turn right. Step out along a gated road towards Halton East from where there are good views across pastures to Halton Height. Take the first right turn - Moor Lane. After forty yards turn left, in front of several cottages, along a signposted path to Eastby. Pass through a stone stile and then head diagonally right to a gate into a farmyard. Here, swallows fly in and out of the barns and gather on overhead wires.

Walk through the farm, turn left and walk to an orange gate. Beyond stride across a meadow and pass through three stiles to a track coming from a farm. Cross the track and walk to the right corner, to a stile obscured, in September, by foliage. Walk on, diagonally right again, to the next stile in the far corner. Beyond, follow a wide track to a gate to Bark Lane. This old walled track is a joy to walk. It is lined with hawthorn, rose, sycamore, ash and bramble. In the verge blue cranesbill flowers.

Bark Lane leads to the road to Eastby. Walk on through the village, passing Hunters Croft. Once you have passed the last house on the left look for a tarmac field path on the left. This leads to the church and the footpath back to the car park.

'this . . . grassy track, where mushrooms grow'

91

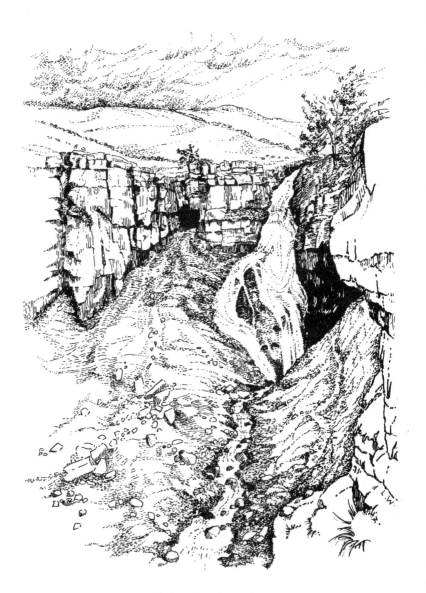

Fall above Yew Cogar Cave

18. Circular walk from Arncliffe, visiting the waterfall high above Yew Cogar Cave

MR 908697, 7½ miles

THIS WALK STARTS at Arncliffe in the depths of the lovely Littondale. Park beside St Oswald's Church. Beyond the car park stands a double-arched bridge over the River Skirfare, just after it has been joined by Cowside Beck. Cross the bridge to see Bridge End, the house where Charles Kingsley gained his inspiration for *The Water Babies*.

Return and walk past the parking area, the church and the school to the village green. Grey stone houses and cottages line the wide grassy area where once sheep and cattle were penned to protect them from the marauding Scots. Turn right and continue to the Falcon Inn. There are no disfiguring bed and

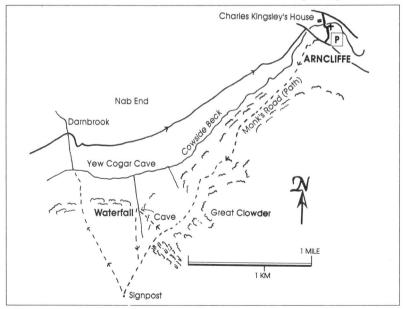

'a double arched bridge over the Skirfare'

breakfast boards outside the cottages - perhaps because the village was the original setting for Emmerdale Farm. Take the signposted public footpath on the far left of the inn, named Monk's Road (path) on the OS map. Follow the walled farm track, lined with yellow balsam and sheltered by scattered ash, to a signposted wicket gate that gives access to the fell.

Begin the steady climb over grassy pastures with limestone outcrops, pausing to enjoy the magnificent view into Littondale. Climb the ladder stile, the first of many that take you over the sturdy limestone walls. These run athwart the fell and down to the Cowside, far below. Continue ascending, using the clear path. Look down to the right to where the valley widens about the meandering beck. Meadow pipits flit about the boulders. Eyebright and tormentil, in mid-September, colour the greensward.

Stride on, keeping well away from the cliff edge to another ladder stile high up to the left. The path beyond climbs gently upwards and then continues over limestone barely covered with turf to the next ladder stile, soon to be followed by another.

Beyond, the path, as it passes below Great Clowder, is well cairned. You are led clearly over the high moorland into an area of dramatic limestone formations and to a ladder stile. Ravens fly overhead 'pruk, pruking' as they go. Follow the path as it swings to the left, encompassing a steep tree-lined gill running down to the beck, and then on to the next ladder stile.

Continue along the ill-defined path, following more cairns. Just before reaching the next stile, begin to drop steadily down the slopes to the right to see the waterfall. The beck, having flowed quietly over the pasture, suddenly descends in a magnificent flared skirt of foaming white water, tumbling with great haste, down tufa-covered rock to the bottom of the deep, sheer-sided gorge. From here the dancing beck hurries in a silver stream to join Cowside Beck.

Cross the beck and pass through a stone gap stile. Turn right and walk a few yards to a large piece of limestone pavement. From here there are excellent views into the striking canyon. Rowan and ash grow about the sides and in the crevices lush gardens of water mint, golden rod, harebells, ferns, knapweed and rushes thrive. To the left of the magnificent waterfall lies a huge, shallow cave where grow a variety of pretty ferns.

To re-gain the footpath walk uphill beside the beck. Where the beck disappears continue ahead. Look left to see the now familiar and reassuring cairns. On reaching the path, turn right and walk on to the next ladder stile. Beyond, a small tarn lies to the right. To the left stand more dramatic limestone escarpments. Follow the now clear bridlepath until you reach a two-armed signpost. Here turn right and take the clear footpath to Darnbrook. This passes through more interesting limestone formations to another ladder stile.

Beyond, the path is indistinct, but keep below the rough ground to the right, dropping steadily downhill, to a gate in a wall. Away to the right of the gate lies an extensive area of limestone pavement. Beyond the gate, walk downhill through a dry gill. Then follow the grassy track as it swings first to the right and then to the left, dropping steeply to the footbridge over Cowside Beck and to a ladder stile over a wall.

Walk ahead to a gap in another wall and on to a metal gate. Continue to a wooden gate and turn right onto the narrow, gated road to Arncliffe. Pass the farm at Darnbrook and follow the very steep hairpin bends uphill to Nab End. Walk on along the glorious lane, from where you can see the spectacular waterfall and the cave and perhaps glimpse Yew Cogar Cave if you move onto the grassy slopes on the right. Continue along this marvellous high level way, with good views of the steep sides of the river valley. As you walk towards the village it is very rewarding to be able to pick out the path taken earlier.

The lane passes a teashop just before reaching the village green and here a restorative cup of tea completes a grand trek.

Golden rod

Falls at Cray

19. Waterfalls at Cray, Crook Gill and Buckden

MR 945797 - 943798 - 934792 - 946775, 6 miles

AUTUMN, YORKSHIRE DALES, Wharfedale, Buckden, Cray, Hubberholme and waterfalls - what lovely words to put together and to conjure with. In whatever order they are arranged the result is near perfection of colour, form and shape. A circular walk in autumn to visit the waterfalls near to these lovely Yorkshire villages commences at Buckden at the northern end of Wharfedale. Here there is a good car park with toilets.

Leave the car park by a stony path that climbs steeply northwards below Buckden Pike. Below to the left hawthorn trees carry a large crop of crimson berries, only slightly redder than their leaves. Horse-chestnut trees catch the sunlight, which turns their leaves to a bright gold. Further to the left, beyond the River Wharfe, the walled pastures, with their abundant scattering

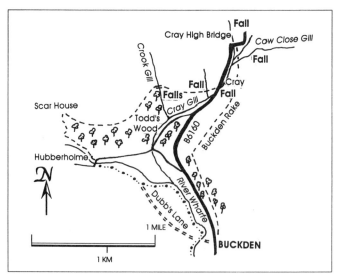

of barns, stretch upwards to the bleak fell.

Follow the track as it passes through the ash, sycamore, hazel and rowan of Rakes Wood. Once beyond the trees the way lies across the open fell, with a sturdy drystone wall to the left and rocky outcrops to the right. Where the path divides walk straight ahead to a gate where a signpost directs the way to Cray High Bridge. A grassy bridleway continues beyond the gate and from here there is a grand bird's-eye view of the waterfall by the bridge. Continue along bridleway, passing the opening in the wall to the path leading down to Cray.

Continue ahead along the distinct path as it gently descends towards the bridge. Overhead a pair of late house martins circle and dive after insects, also on the wing and encouraged forth by the warm October sun. Just before the last gate on the walk to the bridge pass through a gap in the wall. Cross, diagonally, the pasture beyond to the foot of a magnificent waterfall. Here the beck, after racing through Cow Close Gill, drops beneath two guardian ash trees in a long elegant fall onto a series of ledges that cause the water to foam and spray.

Return to the gate and this time pass through, beneath ash, and cross the pastures to the gate above the bridge. This gives access to the road (B6160). Turn left and walk the few steps to the bridge. From here there is an excellent view of another elegant

Cray - beautiful old church of St. Michael's and All Angels

waterfall, but though it is so near to the road there is no public access to its foot. Here the Cray Beck tumbles over a small depression in an amphitheatre of gritstone to a small ledge. It then drops downwards onto another protruding ridge. Finally, at last unimpeded, the Cray descends in a huge cascade that is tugged by the wind, catching the spray and tossing it wantonly into the large semi-circular hollow of rock, away from the fall. A kestrel that has been diligently quartering the fell

Waterfall at Cray on Cray Beck

comes down to the rock just above the edge of the rim and immediately it is lost to sight as its colouring blends with the gritstone.

Walk down the lane, enjoying the lively beck, with its many pretty falls, now racing along on the left. It hurries beneath ash and rowan, the latter covered with multicoloured leaves. Just before the inn take the signposted footpath on the right. This passes between farm buildings and comes to a ford. Upstream the beck descends a scarp beneath ash and sycamore and then descends to the ford in a series of wide limestone steps over which the beck cascades in a mass of white foam. (Make a mental note here to look for the foaming waterfall on the same stream, deep in the trees edging the road in front of the buildings, on your return drive out of the dale.)

Keep to the upper path beyond the ford, following the signpost directions, at the gate, for Yockenthwaite. Here ragwort, hardheads, yarrow, dandelions and buttercups still flower. Follow the path (just a browning of the grass) as it swings across meadows where black cattle chew their cud and jackdaws probe the turf for insects. Beyond the last gate lies Todd's Wood, its brightly coloured deciduous trees covering steep slopes. Cross the beck, which has tumbled in so many sparkling falls through Crook Gill, by a plank bridge. Once under this the racing beck leaps in one long white jet into a leafy hollow before raging on in more falls. Several elms lean gracefully over the lively beck, their leaves now a pale saffron.

Continue along the indistinct path across springy turf. To the left lie large areas of limestone pavement beyond which the tree-clad slopes of Hubberholme Wood drop steeply to the village of the same name and the River Wharfe. Through gaps in the beeches, ash and hazels Wharfedale and its wide stately river can be seen - the river surging beneath trees on the bank now fully arrayed in their autumn garb.

When Scar House is reached turn left as directed by a signpost and walk between the buildings following a stony path that leads steeply downhill. This passes below the trees and joins the Dales Way leading into Hubberholme. This lovely hamlet, with its beautiful old church of St Michael's and All Angels, sits beside the Wharfe. Visit the ancient church and savour its quiet peacefulness and pleasantness, a pleasantness written about by J.B.Priestley whose ashes lie nearby.

Cross the bridge beyond the church and turn left walking along Dubb's Lane. To the right in a meadow a pair of pheasants still care for their noisy brood. Half a mile along the lane take the signposted path on the left which crosses a meadow to come to the side of the Wharfe. It is a joy to walk beside the river where the green leaves of ash contrast sharply with the lemon-coloured leaves of sycamore and the many tones of red of hawthorn and rowan.

When the road is reached turn left, crossing the wide sturdy bridge into Buckden. Keep to the left side of the village green and walk uphill using the alleyways between the gritstone houses until a gate is reached that gives access - a rather muddy access - to the bank of Buckden Beck. Walk up beside the beck to where it descends a long rock slide in a mass of white foam. Leaning over the water are two hawthorn trees laden with berries. These

delight a host of excited blackbirds. Upstream, the beck falls in white-topped cascades as it descends a series of wide limestone steps.

'Yarrow and buttercups still flower'

'the beck . . . drops in sparkling cascades' (Walk 20)

103

20. *Waterfall near Wharfe, starting at Clapham and returning via Austwick*
MR 787693, 8 miles

T HERE IS AMPLE parking in the national park centre at
Clapham. Turn right out of the car park and walk through
the attractive village street beneath beech and horse-chestnut,
now clad in glorious gold and bronze leaves. More leaves line the
gutters. Continue to the front of St James's Church. Walk right
to the large iron gates of Ingleborough Hall (an outdoor education
centre).

Follow the signpost directions for Austwick and walk along a
wide walled track which leads to two longish tunnels. These were
constructed when the hall was built by the Farrer family; the
owners could reach their woodland without having to see the
users of this once busy bridleway (Thwaite Lane).

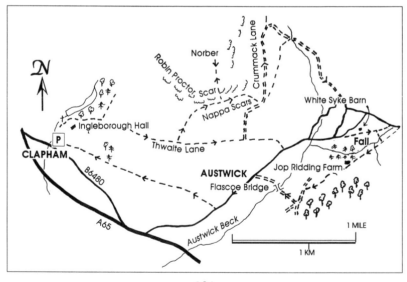

Ladder stile

Beyond the tunnels continue along the walled lane, from where you can hear the ducks on the artificial lake and the splashing of the waterfall as Clapham Beck tumbles into the village. After climbing for a short distance continue along the good track as it passes through riotously coloured deciduous woodland.

Where the track branches, on the edge of the woodland, take the right fork in the direction of Austwick. The wide walled track is edged with scattered hawthorns loaded with dark red berries. Away to the left rise the sheer limestone walls of the oddly named Robin Proctor's Scar - legend has it that Mr Proctor and his horse fell over the edge after a bout of drinking.

Half a mile along the track take the signposted ladder stile on the left and follow the greensward track as it veers to the right to the side of a wall. Continue to another ladder stile and walk on beyond, following the track as it climbs gently to a two-armed signpost. Here a kestrel, mobbed by several jackdaws, eventually retires from the limestone walls and flies off over the pasture land below to the right. Note the position of the signpost because you will need to return to it later. Turn left and walk up the steepish ill-defined track to Norber, a bleak, desolate area of huge gritstone boulders littered over the limestone. These are the famous Norber erratics, carried by an ancient glacier from Crummack Dale and deposited on the Great Scar limestone -

much younger in geological terms. Wander at will and then return down the path, edged with tiny pink cranesbill, harebells, asplenium fern and herb robert, to the signpost.

Walk on, eastwards, in the direction of Crummack, keeping the fell wall to your right. Ascend the rough path below more huge erratics, which appear to teeter on the edge of the limestone wall, to a ladder stile over the wall. Cross the pasture, where the kestrel now tangles with an angry mistle thrush. Continue along the path below the magnificent Nappa Scars, beneath ash trees laden with keys. Walk on to Crummack Lane and turn left. Stride out along this grand walled track, which is lined with hawthorn, elder and rose, laden with berries. Rust-red bracken covers the slopes to the left and, above, limestone scars flare upwards.

At the branching of the track turn right, following the signpost directions for Wharfe. Cross the foaming Austwick Beck on the narrow footbridge and enjoy this quiet corner of Yorkshire. Steep limestone slopes tower to the left and here dozens of fieldfare feed ravenously on the scattered fruit-laden hawthorns. Step out along the delightful walled path until reaching the small hamlet of Wharfe.

Follow the track as it veers slightly to the left and then straightens as it passes between buildings. Stride on to the lane leading to Austwick. Turn left, cross the road and take the footpath signposted White Syke Barn. Cross the stile and walk

'a bleak, desolate area of huge gritstone boulders'

106

ahead beside the wall. Beyond the barn the path crosses the pasture, diagonally right, to a gap in the wall. Keep beside the fence. Below, the beck hurries along the bottom of a deep gill. Through the elm and larch lining the slopes you can glimpse the lovely waterfall dropping steeply down - but hurry on because there is a better view later on the walk.

Continue upstream, pass through a gap in the wall, turn right and cross the beck by a footbridge. Just below, the beck, divided by a huge boulder, drops in sparkling cascades. Through the yellow leaved ash, overhanging the fall, pass several chattering blue tits. Keep above the beck and walk downstream to a ladder stile in the wall. Cross the pasture to another stile giving access to a farm track. Turn right.

Walk beside the fence enclosing a small planting of conifers. Where the trees end look across the gill to the splendid waterfall. From here you can see it in all its glory racing down the great drop in its bed. Each droplet catches the sunlight, making the golden leaves of the larch and the elms suddenly seem dull.

Return to the farm track and walk on to Jop Ridding Farm. Continue in front of the dwelling, following the clear stiled way until reaching Wood Lane, another pleasing walled track. Away to the left another dramatic limestone scar rises steeply.

At the crossroads of tracks leave Wood Lane and follow a signposted track to Flascoe Bridge beside the ford over Austwick Beck. Here you might be tempted to pause once more to enjoy the quiet charm of another glorious corner. Walk on to the Austwick road. Turn left and dawdle through the attractive village. Keeping the village cross and the church to your left, walk on to the signposted footpath to Clapham. It lies on the right, beyond a house named Beech Croft - the leaves of the said beech now bronze and gold.

Follow the stiled footpath across the terraced pastures, marked on the OS map as ancient field systems. After passing through two metal kissing gates on the Ingleborough Estate, continue ahead to a farm. Look for the enclosed path beside the car park and enter it by a stile in the hedge.

Fall seen from the Pennine Way

21. Waterfall at Brants Gill Head and Hull Pot

MR 813729 - 824745, 5 miles

T URN LEFT OUT of the largish car park in the centre of the village of Horton in Ribblesdale, noticing the unusual road sign on the B6479. Cross the bridge and look left to two more bridges over the wide and stately River Ribble. Turn right in front of the Crown Hotel (named New Inn on the OS map) and take the wide cart track off to the left, signposted the Pennine Way.

Stride out along the reinforced track, one of the many used as drove roads by shepherds, for a third of a mile. Turn right through a metal gate and follow the wall on the right to the head of the gill. Look left to where the beck emerges from a dark cave before descending over its bed through the gill in three glorious falls. The brown water flows fast and as it rages over the rocky drops peat stain streaks the white foam. Overhead tower tall Scots pines, their dark foliage a perfect foil for the golden needles of several graceful larch and the bronze leaves of some stately beeches.

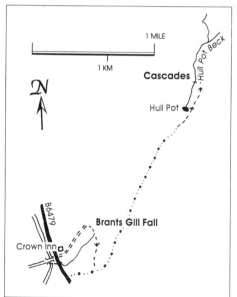

Enjoy this glorious hollow and then return to the tumbledown wall that once bordered the ravine and walk beside it to the right. Look for fossils in the fallen limestone rocks.

Cross the wall ahead by the stone steps and continue right with the ravine below and another view of the falls in Brants Gill Head. Cross the next wall using a rather rickety stone stile and step out across the pasture, through two gates, to another section of the Pennine Way.

Turn left and walk the walled track where it passes beside a small plantation of alder, larch and beech - the leaves of the latter yellow-brown in the late October sunlight. The trees are soon left behind and bleak pastures stretch away on either side with Pen-y-ghent towering upwards on the right. Jackdaws noisily fly over the pastures on their way to the limestone walls of Horton Scar.

Just beyond a gate in the wall on the right, look down to an attractive waterfall. The small stream plummets from a limestone amphitheatre into a small pool. It then descends in pretty cascades to a larger deeper brown basin before flowing through the quiet valley. Follow the track as it moves deeper into the limestone countryside. Ahead can be seen the spectacular Tarn Bar, a Malham Cove in miniature. At the three-armed signpost continue ahead along a wide grassy swathe - the Pennine Way swinging away to the right in the direction of the summit.

Suddenly Hull Pot yawns ahead. Meadow pipits, unconcerned by the chasm, flit about the vegetation that hangs over the edge of the sheer sides of this collapsed cavern. After heavy rain Hull Pot Beck drops in a cloud of spray into the pothole, but when there is less water the beck disappears before the edge. It emerges from a cave two-thirds of the way down the cliff face, where it falls in dancing white-topped cascades and then goes underground. Once, the huge canyon was encircled by a protective wall. This now lies in small heaps of stones and there is no protection; a place to be avoided after dark and in dense mist.

Walk on upstream to where the beck cascades over a series of wide steps in its bed. Look for the dipper that runs into the water after insects and for spearwort brightening the marshy edges of the moorland stream.

Return along the grassy path and then the Pennine Way to Horton, one and a quarter miles. On reaching the road, turn right for the car park or left for St Oswald's, the church on the Pennine Way and in the shadow of Pen-y-ghent. The building dates from the early twelfth century. Look for the dog-tooth patterning on the stone arch over the south doorway and the magnificent Norman pillars and arches in the nave. Notice the lych gates and the huge slabs of slate used for the path between them.

'notice the unusual road sign'

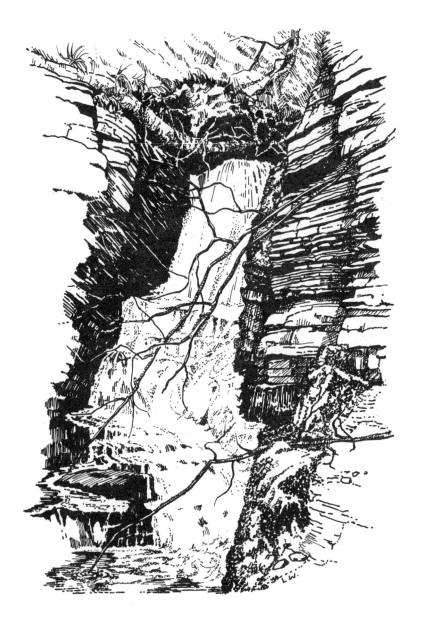

Foss Gill

22. Waterfalls in Foss Gill, Calton and on the River Aire

MR 914597, 7½ miles

T HE YELLOW-GOLD leaves of the elm trees fill Foss Gill with a warm, welcoming glow. Beneath these trees the lively Foss Beck tumbles in a series of glorious waterfalls. After rain the noise of the turbulent stream reverberates from the walls of the narrow gill.

To visit the waterfalls, park in the quiet hamlet of Calton. Where the road signposted Grassington turns sharp right, walk straight ahead (north-east) to the end of the tarmac and descend the bridleway to the stream. If the beck is in spate, off with your boots to cross the ford. Continue along the track on the other side, passing through hazel, hawthorn and elm. Very soon the gated track climbs out of the wood and continues over the moorland to Weets Gate. Before the gate take a path to the right, keeping a wall to your left. The clear path continues through the trees and beside the rushing water.

After a few yards the way leads to a small steep-sided ravine supporting a variety of ferns and bushes. The path comes to the side of the beck and you will have to cross the beck again, either on convenient stones or by wading. Climb the path, continuing on the other side, to view the splendid falls; each one is spectacular and all are different. When you have had your fill of this November splendour, return the same way to the start of the bridleway.

Walk ahead and take the signposted bridleway on the right. This passes between sturdy walls - an old drove road perhaps - to the side of the hurrying beck once more. Fortunately a sturdy sleeper enables you to cross dryshod, but take care - it can be very slippery after rain. Turn left, as directed by the signpost, and walk downstream. The Foss races beneath magnificent beeches, now aglow with bronzed leaves. Just before it joins the River Aire it descends in two pleasing falls.

Follow the indistinct grassy path and as it nears the confluence, bear right to walk upstream beside the River Aire. The footpath keeps well above the surging river, swollen with heavy overnight rain. It passes above more deciduous trees before it begins to drop downhill close to a weir over which the Aire surges with an angry roar. Just beyond, look for the yellow waymarked ladder stile to a footbridge over Crook Syke to join the Pennine Way.

Turn right and stride out along the gated way towards Hanlith, passing through gracious parkland and keeping close to the river. Dippers and mallards frequent the shallows and wrens flit about the riverside vegetation. Pass through the gap stile in the wall before Hanlith Hall and turn left to cross Hanlith Bridge. Turn right to walk the delightful riverside walk to Malham. This passes to the left of Scalegill Mill and then continues beside

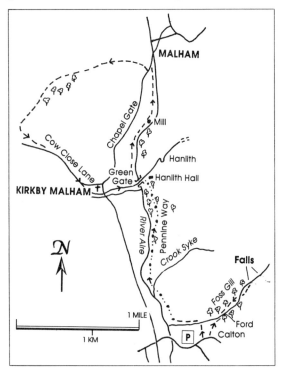

several dams where you can see swans, coots, mallards and moorhens. Hawthorn trees, laden with berries, line the path.

Look ahead for a grand view of Malham Cove and Gordale Scar. Stride out along the stiled way until you reach Malham. Once over the last ladder stile, turn left and cross Chapel Gate. Walk in front of the information centre to Peart Lane, a leaf-strewn walled

114

track that climbs steadily away from the village. Where the lane ends continue ahead following the signpost directions. There is no obvious path but look to see the ladder stiles over the walls ahead. Most of these are faintly waymarked and encourage you on the unrelenting climb. Where the way descends slightly to a footbridge over a stream look for grey squirrels gathering winter stores below lofty beeches.

Continue walking ahead from the footbridge to the next stile. A yellow arrow directs you ahead. Follow it, but be alert because after twenty yards the way swings to the left to a conspicuous ladder stile. This gives access to a farm track. Turn left and walk downhill to the gate to Cow Close Lane. This leads steeply down to Kirkby Malham, between heavily berried hawthorns which delight a large flock of fieldfare.

Walk on into the tiny village, which snuggles peacefully among the autumn trees, passing the church on the right. Turn right at the junction with the Malham Road and continue past several charming old cottages. Turn left beyond the church hall, your way signposted Hanlith Only. Step out along Green Gate and cross Hanlith Bridge. Turn right, passing through the stone step stile to walk once more along the Pennine Way. Retrace your outward journey to your car at Calton.

'grey squirrels gathering winter stores'

Hull Pot

23. Waterfalls in Sell Gill Pot, Hull Pot and Hunt Pot

MR 803744 - 824745 - 826741, 6 miles

PARK IN THE car park at Horton in Ribblesdale. Turn left to cross the bridge over Bants Gill Beck and then right in front of the Crown Hotel. Once you have passed in front of the hotel buildings, turn left along the Pennine Way. Stride the wide track that passes between limestone walls, ignoring the footpath on the right to Brants Gill, taken on the walk to the waterfall (walk 21).

Pen-y-ghent rears, flat-topped and ridged, to the right and, to the left, a large flock of starlings probes the pastures for insects. Beyond lies Ingleborough, its head in the clouds. The way continues muddily and unrelentingly upwards after a gate. Stride on until you come to Sell Gill Holes. Here Sell Gill Beck dances down from the moorland slopes to descend in a white-topped cascade before beginning one continuous foaming drop to the depths below. The limestone overhangs, surrounding the plummeting water, provide a gentler

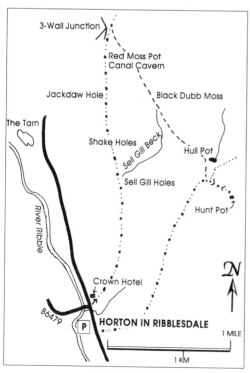

117

environment than on the open fell slopes and here thrive various ferns and flowering plants. On the other side of the path look for the very deep opening into the pot.

Pass through a gate and continue climbing the wide track. Away to the left, down by the River Ribble, lies The Tarn, over which circles a noisy flock of seagulls. Stride on uphill. Look over the wall to a large area of clints and grikes, almost white in the thin winter sunshine. Pass through the next gate and continue along the now grassy way - a pleasing high level path giving good views to more limestone pavement. Look to the right of the path for some very deep shake holes (funnel-shaped depressions).

Leave the path and lean over the boundary wall, on the left, to see Jackdaw Hole, a huge chasm in the limestone surrounded by large ash trees and a solitary Scots pine. Just below the rim of the abyss several young ash have rooted in the crevices, together with a variety of ferns. Ivy, covered with flower heads, trails over the sheer sides and softens the awesome pit.

Walk on past the narrow slit of Red Moss Pot Canal Cavern on the right of the path - you can hear the water falling far below, but this time you cannot

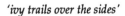

'ivy trails over the sides'

see it. Here you have your first views of Batty Head viaduct strung out between the hills.

Pass through a gateless gateway and walk on to a junction of three walls on the left. Just beyond, a clear stony track climbs the hill on the right. It then drops down to a ford over the narrow beck heard earlier at Canal Cavern. Climb the next steep slope. Here the track, badly eroded, passes through heather and deer grass. At the top of the slope a grand view of Pen-y-ghent lifts the spirits.

Descend the next slope and pass through a gap in the wall. Beyond lies a severely worn area where erosion control is in progress. Once beyond this, do not continue up the wide track ahead which crosses the aptly named Black Dubb Moss, but take a narrow path leading to the right. Apart from one rather wet area close by a curving wall the path leads clearly to a gap in the fell wall. It continues beyond, steadily dropping downhill to the edge of Hull Pot.

If November has been wet you are likely to see Hull Pot Beck coming to the edge of the huge cavern before it descends in a lace-like curtain of water. The beck drops sixty feet in a magnificent

Sell Gill Hole

119

cloud of spray before hurrying away underground.

Walk on to join the Pennine Way, turning left to climb a ladder stile (one or two) over a wall. Beyond, the wide reinforced track begins its steady climb towards the summit of Pen-y-ghent. Just before the next wall and two more stiles, move right away from the track to the edge of Hunt Pot. Here the sparkling beck tumbles in delightful cascades over a long series of ledges. It descends into a wide, grassy oval-shaped hollow strewn with large limestone boulders. It hurries across a flattish area before dropping over a ledge, each droplet silvered by sunlight, into a long, narrow, deep chasm.

Return along the track and cross the twin stiles. Take the signposted left-turn to Horton. At the end of the track, turn right and walk to the car park.

'brilliantly coloured hawthorn berries' (walk 24)

24. Circular walk from Arncliffe, including the waterfall on Sleets Gill Beck

MR 962695, 8 miles

THIS IS A glorious walk for one of those bright November days after several days of rain. The riverside way is a joy. The climb over the tops to Kettlewell, and the even higher climb to return to Arncliffe, afford breathtaking views to be savoured slowly. Park by St Oswald's Church at Arncliffe as for walk number 18. Turn left and walk past the church. There was a stone building here from the eleventh century and this probably superseded a Saxon

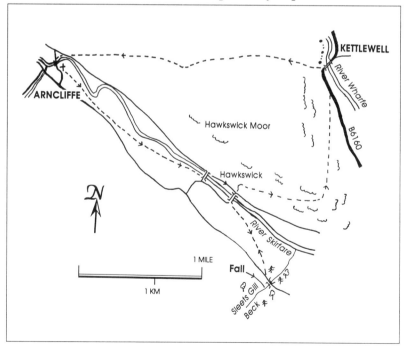

church. The present church was largely re-built in the sixteenth and eighteenth centuries.

Take the signposted footpath on the left, passing between the outbuildings beside the vicarage, to a wicket gate to pastures. To the left flows the River Skirfare - a Danish word for Scots pine - where mallards take flight and head downstream. Pass through a waymarked gate and continue along a high level path above the river. Look for the huge hornbeam leaning over the hurrying water. It carries a large crop of seeds. Each has a three-pronged wing, the middle prong much longer than the other two.

Climb a ladder stile and follow a footpath sign to another. Continue beside a wall with a row of Scots pine away to the left. Pass through two gap stiles to cross the end of a small lane. Pass through another gap stile and stride across the pasture beyond. Look right to the slopes of Blue Scar and left to the limestone scar of Hawkswick Moor - this is the return route.

Pass through a waymarked gate on your right and turn left to walk beside a wall to the riverside. Climb another stile, cross a small stream and the stile beyond. Continue across the meadow to a gate in the distance. Notice the row of hawthorns to the left, laden with brilliantly coloured hawthorn berries, a bright patch of deep red against the white of the limestone scar.

Continue through a gate and cross another ladder stile. The next stile brings you beside the river again, where a dipper sits on a boulder, and pairs of mallards seem to have settled on their reaches of the Skirfare. Cross a wooden footbridge over a dry river bed and walk ahead over pasture. Pass through the next stile and then a wicket gate in a wall. The next stile brings you to a narrow reinforced path beside the river. Step out along the path, which is lined with ash and sycamore, and then cross the river by a sturdy iron bridge. Turn right and walk into the peaceful hamlet of Hawkswick.

At the end of the village, cross the river again by the elegant shallow-arched bridge and turn left along a footpath signposted Arncliffe Road. The reinforced path swings to the right across a meadow to a stile beside a gate. Pass to the right of a wooden bungalow and then take a footpath that turns left off the access road to the bungalow. Look left to the far side of the valley to see

Fall on Sleets Gill Beck

ancient cultivation terraces, lynchets, on the slopes below Hawkswick Moor. Follow the footpath as it bears to the right, keeping a derelict barn to the left. Pass through the signposted gate to Arncliffe Road and turn left. Walk on to Sleets Gill Bridge.

Look right, over the wall to see the waterfall on Sleets Gill Beck marked on the OS map. Unfortunately what should be a raging fall is often dry. To the left a plantation of Scots pine and larch shadows the trickle of water and to the right ash trees grow. In spite of the lack of water the gill is pleasing and the walk grand.

To continue retrace your steps to the stone bridge at Hawkswick. Cross, turn left and take a narrow lane to the right, signposted Kettlewell. Pass through a gate and begin the steady climb, diagonally right and well waymarked, onto Hawkswick Moor. The wide grassy path passes through bracken and comes to a wicket gate. From here there are grand views across to the waterfall, with the Skirfare meandering placidly through the bordering pastures.

Almost a mile from the village, look for the large pile of stones. This is the point, not to be missed, to turn left to a stile over the fell wall. Look right to see Kilnsey Crag and the valley of the River Wharfe. Beyond the stile bear away to the left, following a springy grassy track across limestone pasture. Continue along the clear path and follow it as it begins to descend to a stile into a wood. Here huge Scots pine grow on an extensive ledge of limestone. Follow the rough track as it zig-zags downhill. Keep to the right of a derelict building and follow the waymarked route as it descends. Keep a wall to your left and pass through a waymarked gate into woodland of sycamore and Scots pine. The path leads gently downhill to the B6160. Turn left and walk on to cross New Bridge over the Wharfe. Walk into Kettlewell.

After a quiet browse in this pleasing Dales village return across the bridge and walk to an open area on the right. Take the higher gate on the right (the lower one leads down to the river). Walk along the bridleway, which goes to a farm. After a few yards, leave the farm track and bear to the left, climbing to a waymarked stile. Beyond, continue the inexorable climb to a fissure in the limestone crag. Scramble through the gap. Look for the waymark directly ahead to pick up a rough track. Head slightly to the right, following waymarked stones to a signpost pointing in the direction of Arncliffe. Overhead seagulls glide.

Look right from here to see the villages of Starbotton and Buckden. Climb a ladder stile and continue climbing, following a faint grassy track bearing slightly right to another ladder stile over the fell wall. This is the highest part of the walk. Beyond the stile bear diagonally right, crossing the corner of the pasture, to another ladder stile.

From now on a wide grassy path descends through heather to a two-armed footpath sign. Below, Arncliffe comes into view. Look across to Blue Scar, Yew Cogar Scar and the riverside path taken earlier. Follow the clear path to a ladder stile into Cackle Rash Wood. Take care here when descending the very rough path, keeping to the left of an old wall. The rough track continues downhill through ancient woodland of ash, hazel and hawthorn.

Pass through the gate to a pasture with scattered ash trees. Follow the path right to yet another ladder stile. Beyond, continue downhill to a squeeze stile onto the road. Cross, climb down stone steps and follow the riverside wall. On the opposite bank stands St Oswald's Church. Look for the pretty rapids on the racing river. Climb the steps to the road and turn left to cross the bridge. The car park lies to the left.

Linton Falls

25. Waterfall near Burnsall and Linton Falls

MR 034617 - 002633, 8 miles

THE CAR PARK is situated by the side of the River Wharfe at Burnsall. The narrow village street winds up past the Methodist church and the Church of St Wilfrid and its sixteenth century tower. Beside the church is the primary school, once the grammar school. It has rows of mullioned windows and was built around 1602.

Cross the massive five-arched bridge over the Wharfe, below which mallards swim. Go down the stone steps on the left, signposted Skuff Road. Look for the plaque in the wall that says the bridge was repaired in 1674 and, further to the left, notice the flood tunnel below the road. Pass through a wicket gate and walk beside the river beneath sycamore and ash.

Climb a ladder stile and continue along a narrow, rough path by the side of the stately Wharfe. Just beyond a fence a pretty

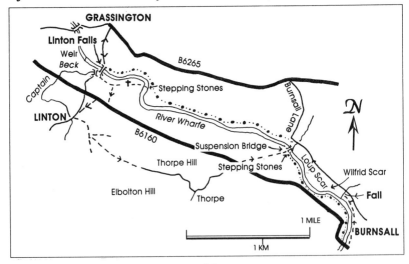

waterfall tumbles down a steep limestone gill, frothing and foaming on its way to join the river. Elm trees line the sides and herb robert flowers along the side of the water. After a dry spell the gill is dry but view it after rain and it is an attractive sight, the haunt of wrens, blue tits and chaffinches.

Return along the path for a dozen yards and take the indistinct path up the slope, following it to a signposted wicket gate onto Burnsall Lane, a continuation of Skuff Road. Turn left and walk towards the cluster of houses about Mill Bridge, with grand views across the valley of the Wharfe. The lane is lined with ash and in one tree several pairs of rooks sit very close.

Cross the bridge and walk on to the two-armed signpost on the left. Strike diagonally right across the pasture to join the Dales Way, walking in the direction of Grassington. Away to the left lies the Hebden suspension bridge, seen closer as you return.

The gated path continues beside the hurrying water, where a dipper runs into the shallows about a boulder. The path passes beneath horse-chestnut trees with fat sticky buds. To the right of the path stands a row of very tall lime trees. The hawthorns along the bank are laden with berries, attracting a host of noisy fieldfares. Linton Church comes into view and then the stepping-stones across the Wharfe - once the route taken by the parishioners of Hebden before the village had its own church.

Climb the stile to a track and continue to where it becomes a tarmac road, passing a building that was once a mill. Walk eighty yards onwards, after crossing a small stream, to a gap stile in the wall to a pasture beyond. Linton Church now lies across the river. Climb the stone steps over a wall, from where the water raging down Linton Falls and

'a signposted wicket gate'

127

Li'le Emily's bridge

the two dams can be heard.

These dramatic falls racing through the craggy, limestone rocks in skirts of lacy foam, occur across the North Craven Fault - which separates the limestones of the north from the more recent millstone grit of the south. Pass through a gap stile to a walled path, known locally as the Snake Walk. Turn right and climb the path to visit Grassington - a handsome Dales village where miners who wrested lead from the moors above the settlement lived.

Return along the Snake Walk and cross the falls on the splendid wooden bridge which has replaced the old tin bridge. Follow the path around to the right to a pack-horse bridge, over Captain Beck, known as Li'le Emily's Bridge. This was used by local folk attending Linton Church. Do not cross the bridge, but continue along the path to the road. Turn left to view the twelfth century church in its secluded setting.

On leaving, walk back along the lane and turn left into a track beyond Holme House. Take the signposted footpath on the right. This narrow reinforced path continues to the main Grassington to Burnsall road. Turn right and then take the left fork to walk into the village of Linton. Here find time to dawdle. Gracious

128

eighteenth and nineteenth houses lie scattered around the large village green. Linton Beck flows through the village and is spanned by a road bridge, a pack-horse bridge and a footbridge. Cross the road bridge and walk beside the green. Turn left to pass in front of the magnificent almshouses - Fountaine Hospital - and cross the beck again by the footbridge.

Turn right and walk towards a farm at the end of the road. Follow the footpath sign to Cracoe and Thorpe. Notice the bee boles in the wall of the farmhouse where basket skips for the bees were placed. Continue along the muddy track, which soon becomes dry once it begins to climb. Look left across the magnificent limestone boundary walls of the pastures above Grassington. Climb the sloping path to a ladder stile and continue to another. Beyond, climb over terraces, once areas of ancient cultivation, to the left side of a small plantation of ash trees. Follow the footpath sign to some stone steps which give access to a narrow road, below Elbolton Hill - a reef knoll, one of a series of dome-shaped limestone hills.

Turn left and then right at the end of the narrow lane, to drop down into the hidden hamlet of Thorpe. Follow the lane round to the left, keeping to the left of the tiny village green. Cross the B6160 and climb the stile, following the waymarked path downhill to the suspension bridge, seen earlier on the walk. Pass through the gate to the riverside path and turn right. Pass the bottom of the postman's steps and continue along the good path. On the far side of the Wharfe a female goosander hunts for fish, swimming underwater like a mini-submarine. Continue, passing Loup Scar with its magnificent layering of rock, and then Wilfrid Scar. Look across for another sighting of the waterfall visited at the start of the walk. Then walk on to the five-arched bridge and into Burnsall.

'bee-boles in the wall

129

Near Bordley Green Farm

26. Walk to the waterfall near Bordley Green Farm
MR 944645, 7 miles

IN THE MIDDLE of December the drive from Stainforth to Street Gate, east of Malham Tarn, can be nerve-racking. The snow, pushed back by the snow plough, stands four feet high on either side of the narrow lanes. Park on a grassy verge at Street Gate and pass through the gate following the signpost directions for Grassington. Walk ahead keeping the wall to the right.

Look right to see the great limestone cliffs at the entrance to Gordale gorge. Snow lies patchily over the moorland slopes and Swaledale sheep graze on scattered green areas. Young rooks probe the ground searching for insects.

Follow the track down the slope to cross Gordale Beck by a small clapper bridge. Pass through the gate and ascend the slope, keeping the wall to the right. Glorious views stretch away in all directions, each wall with great snowdrifts on either side.

Pass through the next gate onto Mastiles Lane, a wide walled

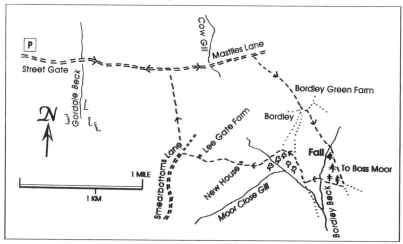

131

drove road. Today the way, part reinforced, part grassy, is covered with three feet of snow, frozen so hard that there is no fear of sinking through. Huge holes in the snow beside the wall show where sheep, huddling in the blizzard, have been dragged to safety. Along the side of the walls a row of neat holes has been drilled by the farmer prodding for survivors. In some places the snow has almost covered the walls and it is possible to walk along the top of the stones without causing damage.

Follow the track downhill into a hollow in the hills. At a four-armed signpost turn right to walk the half mile to Bordley. The wide farm track climbs uphill over rock-strewn moorland. The track then becomes tarmacked and begins to descend towards the farm in its lovely secluded hollow. Several large ash trees lean over the buildings.

Suddenly you pass between six-foot drifts, revealing the intensity of the previous week's blizzard. Pass a deserted cottage on the right and then take a well-signposted track on the left in the direction of Boss Moor. Walk along a muddy track, passing penned cattle, to a gate. Walk on towards the trees in the distance. Cross the gated stream that hurries over the track and then climb the slope ahead. Pass through a gate. Here leave the track and walk down the slope on the right, keeping close to the wall. Pass to the right of a derelict barn and drop down the slope to a gap in the wall. From here there is a grand view of the pretty waterfall.

Bordley Beck passes under a wall, surges round a huge boulder and then tumbles in long lace-like streamers. It falls into a small gorge where ash, sycamore and Scots pine grow along the top of the limestone scar and on the sheer slopes. The hurrying water bounces onto ledge after ledge until it nears the bottom, where it falls in a glorious cascade. It dances through the copse, its banks lined with snow, and continues towards Bordley Hall.

Leave this quiet sheltered corner, return to the track and continue towards a plantation of firs. At the end of the trees a signpost directs you right, downhill, for half a mile to Bordley Hall. Look for the waymark pointing to the ford on Bordley Beck. Just upstream are some convenient boulders for the crossing. Look left to see the culverted wall that allows the beck to continue on its way.

Follow the waymark pointing uphill, keeping the wall and barns to your left. At the five-armed signpost, take the right turn to Bordley Town. Beyond the gate walk uphill over a large pasture to a gap in the wall ahead. Beyond bear left and pass through a wide gap in a wall following a faint track. Continue, keeping a tumbledown wall on the right, to a wooden gate. Beyond turn left, keeping beside the wall, and where this swings away to the left, dropping steeply downhill, follow the path as it keeps above the attractive tree-lined Cow Gill. The path drops steadily downhill to the beck. Cross the small stream and climb up the slope to cross a stile in the wall.

Turn right to walk uphill and pass through a gate on the right. Strike over right in front of New House and continue through a farm gate, passing through farm buildings. Here a farmer told the writer about the earlier blizzard and of many sheep that had died.

Walk up the walled lane and cross the cattle-grid. Stride out along the farm track and cross another grid. Lee Gate Farm lies to the right. Pass through the farmyard, where more huge snowdrifts lie very close to the buildings. To the left dozens of starlings sit on the roof of a barn, chattering noisily in the thin winter sunshine. Walk on until reaching Smearbottoms Lane. Cross over and walk ahead for just over half a mile, keeping a wall to your left. A gate gives access to the track just above Gordale Beck, crossed earlier. To cross the gate takes just a step when hard-packed snow lies two feet high on either side.

Turn left and walk back to the bridge over the beck and continue on to Street Gate.

'culverted wall'

Blea Gill Fall

134

27. Walk around Grimwith Reservoir and to Blea Gill Waterfall

MR 045661, 5 miles

G RIMWITH RESERVOIR lies to the east of Grassington.
Continue along the B6265 through Hebden and cross
Dibble's Bridge. The approach road, on the left, to the parking
area beside the reservoir, is well signposted. There are good toilet
facilities with hot water and radiators and overlooking the water
are a dozen picnic tables.

To take the anticlockwise route around the reservoir, turn
right to walk along a wide track to a gate. The reservoir lies to the
left, with delightful reflections of a moorland farm and of the
surrounding snow-covered hillside. Keep to the high-level track,

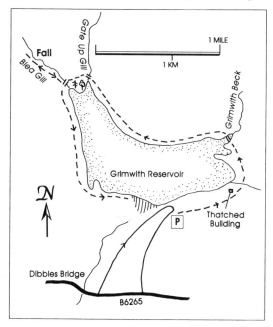

which gives good views, over the wall, of heather moorland, from where grouse call. Stride out along the track to pass a single-storey building thatched with heather, bilberry and moss. Courting mallards call from the nearby still water.

Look for the small areas close to the track that have been planted with ash, alder, birch and firs. These mixed copses, sympathetically planned, break up the severity of the winter moorland. Look, too, for the dipper, hunting for insects in one of the many feeder streams.

A heron flies lazily over the water. Earlier, we disturbed it as it fed quietly in the shallows. Walk on along the wide track past a derelict farm building and a large barn. Pass through a kissing gate and walk on along a narrow, indistinct path. This is rough in parts, passing between boulders. It can be very muddy after snow and rain. Cross a narrow plank bridge over a narrow beck, which falls in white-topped cascades beneath a series of snow bridges.

Suddenly the air is filled with the noisy gossiping of a flock of barnacle geese. As they land on the reservoir they make a loud shushing noise. The narrow path leads to another kissing gate and beyond continues as a wide track where walking is easier. Cross the beck hurrying down Gate Up Gill by a sturdy wooden bridge. The peat-stained water rages round boulders on its way to the reservoir. Beyond the bridge the track climbs uphill and to the left lies a large planting of deciduous and coniferous trees.

Cross the next bridge over Blea Beck and pass through the gate on the right side of the track. Follow a narrow, faint path that climbs through the gill, keeping to the left side of the racing beck. Small side streams can be crossed by a single step. The path passes between boulders and over humps and sometimes comes close to the foaming water. Then, as you reach the last fold in the sheer sides of the ravine, the skirt of the waterfall is viewed. With each step more and more is seen until at last the full majesty of Blea Gill Waterfall is revealed.

Forty feet up the torrent roars over the lip of a gritstone amphitheatre. It descends in a lacy cascade onto ledges, then drops in two peat-stained jets to be re-united as a huge skirt of water that plummets into a deep, dark, seething basin. The sheer sides of the canyon, black from the splashing water, bounce the noise of the hurtling beck from side to side. Where there are ledges lush vegetation grows. Here, in contrast to the wintry fells, thrive a multitude of ferns, mosses, liverworts and flowering plants, luxuriating in the sheltered environment of the ravine.

Return down the gill to the gate. Beyond, turn right and continue along the wide track. To the left the geese still feed. At a three-armed signpost turn left to walk beside a barn with a cobbled area in front. Walk on along a wide green swathe to climb a ladder stile. Continue, keeping the reservoir to the left and a wall to the right. Climb a stone-stepped stile and step out over the springy turf, keeping the man-made blocks to your left. These form the embankment of the reservoir. Pass through a gate onto a metalled road. Turn left to walk to the car park.

'a building thatched with heather'

Catrigg Force

28. Stainforth Force and Catrigg Force, Stainforth
MR 818673 - 833671, 4½ miles

A PERFECT DECEMBER day dawns. The sun comes up surrounded by soft pink clouds that stretch across the sky. Beyond the pink the bluest of blue skies reflects such a light as to drag the most reluctant from their beds. Once up, walkers are beckoned invitingly by the Yorkshire waterfalls.

The A65 by-passes Kirkby Lonsdale, Ingleton and Clapham but does not by-pass the glories of the lovely rolling countryside. You can enjoy the bright green grass and the limestone walls that march across the fells. The trees, now bereft of their leaves, allow unimpeded views of Ingleborough and Pen-y-ghent, startlingly

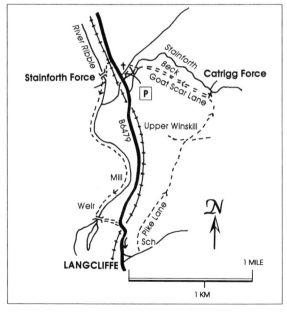

'bullfinches flit through the branches'

clear in the bright sunlight.

Cross the Ribble on the outskirts of Settle and turn left along the B6479. After two and a half miles turn right into the village of Stainforth, parking in the car park on the right, just off the main road. After parking return to the B6479, cross the road and walk on 200 yards, taking a narrow left-hand turn that leads down a narrow lane. Here, where the lane swings to the left, a pair of bullfinches flits through the bare branches of the hedge calling quietly to each other.

The lane then crosses the Ribble by a narrow pack-horse bridge. Do not attempt this way by car in summer; the lane has virtually no passing places and the bridge provides only an inch or two clearance. At the far side of the bridge climb through a gap in the wall on the left. Sturdy steps lead down to the narrow riverside walk. From here look back to the bridge, reflected in the surging brown water.

A short walk brings you to the edge of Stainforth Force, where the Ribble falls over narrow limestone steps before racing over a shallow, wide ledge. It rages on to descend a much steeper fall in a flurry of foam, streaked with sienna, into a deep black pool. Beyond, the river widens and flows leisurely over its rock bed. On the far side of the water a narrow wood of beech, oak and sycamore plays host to a troop of chattering coal tits and several young chaffinches. Overhead a buzzard, wheeling lazily in the blue sky, the sun catching its striking garb, is reluctant to leave its sunbathing for several troublesome crows that wish it on its way.

Continue along the path, climbing a ladder stile into a wide

140

'chattering coaltits'

flat pasture. From here there are grand views of green fells occasionally shadowed as clouds scud over the sun. Walk on along this glorious riverside path, which is part of the Ribble Way and is stiled. Generally it runs just above the racing river. It soon comes close to a mill where paper is recycled. Keep on until reaching a magnificent weir. Cross the foaming water by the narrow footbridge. Look for the fish pass, which allows trout and salmon to by-pass the turbulent water.

Turn left, beyond the bridge, and walk the narrow lane to the B6479. Turn right and walk a hundred yards to the edge of Langcliffe village. Turn left and walk between the attractive cottages to the large village green. Look for a seat encircling the trunk of a large sycamore - this is the place for your picnic.

Leave the green in the direction of the school and just before the building take a left turn along a reinforced track. Follow this as it veers to the right and leads out of the village. This is Pike Lane, a walled track. Pink yarrow and herb robert flower in the grassy verge and the track is a joy to walk. Look across to the fine, limestone face of Stainforth Scar.

Pass through the gate and continue ahead along

a raised grassy track to the top left corner of the park-like pasture. Here the track is walled but, alas, the walls are derelict. The greensward way climbs steadily upwards coming close to fenced woodland. Climb the path beside the trees to a small gate.

Beyond, climb the steepish slope. There is no clear path but walk straight ahead until you reach a ladder stile on the left. Once over turn right and cross the pasture to another stile onto a walled lane. Turn right and stride on until you reach the signpost to Catrigg Force at the junction of tracks, close to the buildings at Upper Winskill.

The track in the direction of the force is clear at first. Where it becomes indistinct continue ahead until reaching a signposted gate on the left. Pause here and enjoy the glorious view of Ingleborough, Fountains Fell and Pen-y-ghent. Pass through the gate and drop downhill, aiming for the ladder stile in the bottom left corner. Then take a second ladder stile close-by on the right that gives access to Goat Lane. Climb a third ladder stile opposite and walk down the path (very slippery after rain) to a grassy hollow. Ahead lies the edge of the immensely deep gorge. Once the treacherous rim was fenced but now the wire and posts lie on the ground. (Care is required with children and pets.)

Cross the stile on the left. It leads to an often muddy, railed track which drops downhill through a magnificent beech wood. It curves round and then swings to the right into a hollow. The glorious Catrigg Force (one of the grandest in Craven) is revealed so suddenly as to be quite breathtaking.

Stainforth Beck plunges over a precipitous lip in a double fall that streams like white lace into a deep hollow where the water foams and sprays behind huge boulders. It then surges between two constraining rocks to fall in graceful cascades into a shadowy basin. The force is majestic when in spate and spray covers the flat rocks about the banks. These can become very slippery.

Over the years the dark brown water has undermined the sheer limestone sides of the ravine. High at the top of the rock walls the sun shines brightly on the grey trunks of larch laden with cones and beech heavily burdened with mast. The sides of the lovely hollow are green with polypody fern, hart's tongue fern and saxifrage and the woodland floor is carpeted with bronze

142

leaves. Blue tits hunt along the branches for insects.

Return through the trees along the railed and stepped path to Goat Lane. Turn right and step out along the walled lane which drops steeply downhill into Stainforth. Walk into the village. To the right you can cross Stainforth Beck (if not in spate) by a fine row of stepping-stones to a green on the other side. If these are under water, continue on and turn right. Turn right opposite the public house called the Craven Heifer, and follow the lane round to the right past the Church of St Peter. Here, atop a large yew, sits a mistle thrush singing a clear, sweet song as if in defiance of weather and visitor alike, a lovely sound in the depth of winter. From the church it is a short walk, left, to the car park.

'woodland floor carpeted with bronze leaves'

143

CICERONE GUIDES

Cicerone publish a wide range of reliable guides to walking and climbing in Britain, and other general interest books.

LAKE DISTRICT - General Books
LAKELAND VILLAGES
LAKELAND TOWNS
WORDSWORTH'S DUDDON REVISITED
THE REGATTA MEN
REFLECTIONS ON THE LAKES
OUR CUMBRIA   PETTIE
THE HIGH FELLS OF LAKELAND
CONISTON COPPER A History
LAKELAND - A taste to remember (Recipes)
THE LOST RESORT?
CHRONICLES OF MILNTHORPE
LOST LANCASHIRE
THE PRIORY OF CARTMEL

LAKE DISTRICT - Guide Books
CASTLES IN CUMBRIA
WESTMORLAND HERITAGE WALK
IN SEARCH OF WESTMORLAND
CONISTON COPPER MINES Field Guide
SCRAMBLES IN THE LAKE DISTRICT
MORE SCRAMBLES IN THE LAKE DISTRICT
WINTER CLIMBS IN THE LAKE DISTRICT
WALKS IN SILVERDALE/ARNSIDE
BIRDS OF MORECAMBE BAY
THE EDEN WAY

NORTHERN ENGLAND (outside the Lakes
THE YORKSHIRE DALES A walker's guide
WALKING IN THE SOUTH PENNINES
WALKING IN THE NORTH PENNINES
LAUGHS ALONG THE PENNINE WAY
WALKS IN THE YORKSHIRE DALES (3 VOL)
WALKS TO YORKSHIRE WATERFALLS
MORE WALKS TO YORKSHIRE WATERFALLS
NORTH YORK MOORS Walks
THE CLEVELAND WAY & MISSING LINK
DOUGLAS VALLEY WAY
THE RIBBLE WAY
WALKS ON THE WEST PENNINE MOORS
WALKING NORTHERN RAILWAYS EAST
WALKING NORTHERN RAILWAYS WEST
HERITAGE TRAILS IN NW ENGLAND
BIRDWATCHING ON MERSEYSIDE
THE LANCASTER CANAL
FIELD EXCURSIONS IN NW ENGLAND
ROCK CLIMBS LANCASHIRE & NW
THE ISLE OF MAN COASTAL PATH
CANOEISTS GUIDE TO THE NORTH EAST

DERBYSHIRE & EAST MIDLANDS
WHITE PEAK WALKS - 2 Vols
HIGH PEAK WALKS
WHITE PEAK WAY
KINDER LOG
THE VIKING WAY
THE DEVIL'S MILL (Novel)
WHISTLING CLOUGH (Novel)
WALES & WEST MIDLANDS
THE RIDGES OF SNOWDONIA
HILLWALKING IN SNOWDONIA
HILL WALKING IN WALES (2 Vols)
ASCENT OF SNOWDON
WELSH WINTER CLIMBS
SNOWDONIA WHITE WATER SEA & SURF
SCRAMBLES IN SNOWDONIA
ROCK CLIMBS IN WEST MIDLANDS
THE SHROPSHIRE HILLS A Walker's Guide
SOUTH & SOUTH WEST ENGLAND
WALKS IN KENT
THE KENNET & AVON WALK
THE WEALDWAY & VANGUARD WAY
SOUTH DOWNS WAY & DOWNS LINK
COTSWOLD WAY
WALKING ON DARTMOOR
EXMOOR & THE QUANTOCKS
SOUTH WEST WAY - 2 Vol
SCOTLAND
SCRAMBLES IN LOCHABER
SCRAMBLES IN SKYE
THE ISLAND OF RHUM
CAIRNGORMS WINTER CLIMBS
THE CAIRNGORM GLENS (Mountainbike Guide)
WINTER CLIMBS BEN NEVIS & GLENCOE
SCOTTISH RAILWAY WALKS
TORRIDON A Walker's Guide
SKI TOURING IN SCOTLAND

THE MOUNTAINS OF ENGLAND & WALES
VOL 1 WALES
VOL 2 ENGLAND

Also a full range of EUROPEAN guide-books - walking, long distance trails, scrambling, ice-climbing, rock climbing, and other adventurous pursuits.

Other guides are constantly being added to the Cicerone List.
Available from bookshops, outdoor equipment shops or direct (send s.a.e. for price list) from
CICERONE, 2 POLICE SQUARE, MILNTHORPE, CUMBRIA, LA7 7PY

Printed by
Martins of Berwick